THE GREAT
RIP-OFF
IN AMERICAN EDUCATION

THE GREAT
RIP-OFF
IN AMERICAN EDUCATION

UNDERGRADS UNDERSERVED

———DR. MEL SCARLETT———

 **Prometheus Books**

59 John Glenn Drive
Amherst, New York 14228-2197

Published 2004 by Prometheus Books

Inquiries should be addressed to
Prometheus Books
59 John Glenn Drive
Amherst, New York 14228–2197
VOICE: 716–691–0133, ext. 207
FAX: 716–564–2711
WWW.PROMETHEUSBOOKS.COM

08 07 06 05 04   5 4 3 2 1

Library of Congress Cataloging-in-Publication Data

Scarlett, Mel, 1920–
    The great rip-off in American education : undergrads underserved / Mel Scarlett.
      p. cm.
    Includes bibliographical references and index.
    ISBN 1–59102–031–X (alk. paper)
    1. Education, Higher—Aims and objectives—United States. 2. Educational accountability—United States. I. Title.

LA227.4.S33 2003
378.73—dc21
                                       2003041393

Printed in the United States of America on acid-free paper

CONTENTS

PART TWO: DOGMATIC, RADICAL RECOMMENDATIONS FOR REFORM

PART THREE: WRAPPING IT ALL UP

INTRODUCTION

I n the early 1980s, America's schools—kindergarten through high school—were in a terrible state, as revealed in books such as *A Nation at Risk* and *Why Johnny Can't Read*. These and other publications, along with the revelation of declining test scores and some other factors, stimulated a nationwide public outcry for improvement in school systems. States and communities responded, developing comprehensive reform plans, providing significantly increased funding, and launching reform programs in state after state across the country.

In spite of the fact that *A Nation at Risk* contained criticism about colleges and universities as well as K–12, the former seemed to elicit little public concern or action. Higher education, which prepares virtually all the professional personnel for K–12 schools, also received little blame-from the public for the poor performance of K–12; and colleges, schools, and departments of education at best only tinkered and made minimal if any change in their programs for teacher and administrator preparation. Elsewhere within the colleges and universities, there was little perceptible response to the plight and the needs of K–12.

This lack of response is not surprising when viewed in light of the various comprehensive and thorough studies of American higher education—especially undergraduate programs—by knowledgeable groups and individuals which, virtually in chorus, bemoaned the woeful state of higher education. The studies allege that undergraduate education has been in as bad shape as K–12, possibly even worse, and it has not seriously addressed its own problems, let alone provided remedial assistance to K–12.

An interesting question is suggested here: Why have massive elementary and secondary school reform programs been instituted in state after state in response to *A Nation at Risk* and other highly critical evaluations of K–12, while the also highly critical study reports of higher education by prestigious organizations such as the National Institute of Education, the Association of American Colleges, the Carnegie Foundation for the Advancement of Teaching, the Wingspread Group, and the Boyer Commission have stimulated little perceptible response from higher education?

A three-part answer to the question can be provided. First, most of the general public have had experience in K–12, and parents have contacts with the public schools, accounting for most having some knowledge of K–12.

On the other hand, the general public, especially the 75 percent who do not hold bachelor's degrees, know surprisingly little about higher education, according to 1995 studies of what the public thinks of colleges, by the California Higher Education Policy Center and the American Council on Education.

The two studies indicate that, "other than costs, the general public has few complaints about higher education, especially when compared with public schools."

Continuing, "most people don't necessarily hold colleges responsible for students' failure to get a good education. Seventy-one percent of the general public believes that the benefit a student gets from college depends on the effort he or she puts in. If a student doesn't do well at the elementary or secondary level, they put at least part of the blame on the schools; if a student doesn't do well in college, they are much more likely to blame the student."

Taxpayers usually know how much they pay in school taxes, but a great many who didn't attend college and don't have children in college don't even realize that their taxes pay a major share of the costs of educating students in state colleges and universities.

In essence, then, a vast majority of the public have some knowledge of what went on in elementary and secondary schools, while an overwhelming majority have had little understanding of what has transpired in colleges and universities.

Second, *A Nation at Risk* and some other publications critical of K–12 found a large, ready market of somewhat knowledgeable and concerned citizens, and it was to those and other lay citizens that the publications were specifically directed. The resulting groundswell of angry response fueled the vast reform movement.

Most of the general public have little knowledge or concern about how higher education goes about its business, and those who do not realize that their taxes support state colleges and universities would seem to have even less reason for concern about higher education than others. So there was not "a large, ready market" for the studies that were highly critical of higher education.

Additionally, the higher education studies were not prepared for a general market, but instead were designed primarily for the academic community—professors and administrators—often in complex prose and academic jargon.

Understandably, the studies did not generate a groundswell of public support for reform in higher education. But why didn't a responsible academic community respond to the criticisms and recommendations in the studies?

Because, third, for generations America's institutions, colleges, and universities have been among the slowest of America's institutions to change or innovate. Support for this point of view was found in a survey of more than two hundred collegiate institutions by Siegfried, Getz, and Anderson, professors at Vanderbilt University. The results of the survey were presented in the May 19, 1995, *Chronicle of Higher Education* under the heading, "The Snail's Pace of Innovation in Higher Education."

The survey, conducted to find out how quickly the institutions had adopted thirty specific innovations, found that "the average time between the adoption of an innovation by the first institution and its adoption by half of them was more than twenty-five years. Innovations in industry tend to be adopted twice as fast as those in higher education."

Some technological innovations such as automated library catalogues were adopted much more quickly than were academic innovations, and it took an average of forty years for half the institutions in the sample to adopt the five financial innovations included in the study.

Colleges and universities have been described as "organized anar-chies," and the minimal, usually disconnected change that occurs is often the result of what is called "muddling through."

Siegfried, Getz, and Anderson conclude: "top university administra-tors often operate reactively. Their agendas are molded by whoever is suf-ficiently motivated to demand their attention. Short-run problem solving erodes the time available to focus on the 'big picture.' And administra-tors' ability to initiate change is constrained by the academic tradition of collegial decision making."

The various studies that have described the many alleged flaws in higher education have been written in a style and in language that is often difficult for noneducators to comprehend, and therefore, they have not generated a public climate that demands reform.

Colleges and universities are locked into a flawed system that is not organized to facilitate change, and the decision-making philosophy often causes gridlock, preventing or at least slowing change.

And among educators, there does not seem to be a widespread, per-ceived need for the vast, significant change in higher education called for in the highly critical studies.

The obvious conclusion, illustrated by the nonresponse of the past several decades, is that higher education will not undertake major self-examination and reform unless strong, widespread, persistent pressure is brought to bear by an informed, indignant public. Neither the "wake-up" call issued in *An American Imperative* by the Wingspread study group in 1994 nor the forceful Boyer Commission Report in 1998 could bring about the "rethinking of the assumptions of the education enterprise and the reinventing many of its ways of doing business" without the applica-tion of public pressure.

I believe that if this book's stark revelations of the alleged misguided and flagrant malpractice in much of American undergraduate education are effectively communicated to concerned groups—college students, their par-ents, legislators and other state officials, the mass media, potential donors, and other taxpayers—the necessary public pressure can be generated.

Many significant studies and observations of higher education by knowledgeable groups and individuals over the past fifteen years are still relevant because of the slowness of change in higher education, and the studies and observations will be referred to continually throughout this book.

Instead of scholarly, thorough, in-depth discussions, significant points are presented succinctly in a journalistic style in order to be understandable to the general public—so that a great many people across the vast scope of American society will be able to enter into a dialogue about reshaping undergraduate education and will be stimulated to do so.

THE INTENT

The intent of this book is to take an unbiased look—without the defensiveness of a higher education practitioner or the vitriol of an external critic—at American higher education, especially undergraduate education, (1) to ascertain why so many studies say it is not serving the current and future needs of the American society well, and (2) to explore what might be done to improve its performance.

The book does not present a great deal of new research or new knowledge, although it does present a number of new ideas. It is not a model of meticulous, pedantic scholarship, although a great many authoritative sources are utilized. It is deliberately written in a style and language that both educators and noneducators can readily comprehend.

Although recommendations for change are made for virtually all significant aspects of higher education, the book is not intended as a master plan for the reconstruction of higher education.

Assumed trouble spots have been identified, and, drawing on relevant studies and expert comment, some fresh ideas and commonsense suggestions for dealing with trouble spots have been provided. These are intended to be used as a basis for dialogue among higher education practitioners, students, parents of students, governing board members, legislators and other government officials, the press, and other interested and concerned persons.

While there is broad discussion in the book, the suggestions are not presented in an impartial, detached, scholarly manner with many alternatives provided. Rather, there are more than eighty strongly presented specific "radical recommendations," because it is thought that this approach is more likely to stimulate the critical analysis and spirited discussion which are primary aims of the book

While an aroused public is essential to motivate badly needed reform, it is not the intent of this book to stimulate public wrath at individuals or at particular groups—administrators, faculty, board members, etc.

The system is the enemy, and it is the system that will be under attack throughout this book.

There are many faculty and administrators who care about students and student learning. But most have simply slipped into their slots within the system and are acting in accordance with the system. If a reform movement is mounted, many such persons will undoubtedly come to the fore and contribute enthusiastically to the regeneration process and beyond into implementation.

Much of the content in this book will be relevant to both public and private institutions, except for discussions of external governance, where the emphasis is on state institutions, especially those in systems.

ONE

WHAT IF?

W hat if other service businesses treated their customers like many universities treat their undergraduate students?

What if, for example, hospitals dealt with their patients like many universities deal with those seeking a four-year degree?

Suppose a hospital's publicity materials boasted about its nationally famous surgeons and other doctors, its wonderful facilities, and the excellent, caring services it provided for its patients. In the same way, university publicity boasts about its renowned professors and the excellent education it provides for its undergraduate students.

What if you entered the hospital for ligament surgery? And what if the surgeons and the other medical doctors affiliated with the hospital were busy working in the hospital's cancer research center? And what if, therefore, the hospital assigned an intern, inexperienced in surgery and untrained in surgical techniques, to do the surgery? And what if the surgery did not turn out well, and you left the hospital without having received the helpful medical care the hospital's publicity indicated you would receive?

In higher education, a student reads a university's impressive publicity, and enrolls at the institution. He attends classes expecting to meet outstanding professors, but they are off doing research, and inexperienced graduate assistants are assigned to "teach" his classes. The G.A.'s inexperience and their overriding concern about their own graduate studies often result in a very poor "learning" experience for the undergraduate students, many of whom drop out during the first year.

Or, what if you entered the hospital for treatment of pneumonia, and this time a medical doctor was assigned to your case? What if this doctor, as well as the other doctors in the hospital, had studied all about the human body and about diseases, but not about how to provide treatment for a disease—how to cure the patient? And what if the doctor utilized a treatment used hundreds of years ago—applying leeches to your chest to suck out the poison and cure your pneumonia? And what if the leech procedure didn't work and you left the hospital not having received the effective medical care you were led by the hospital's publicity to expect?

It often happens that a student enrolls in a university as an undergraduate and actually finds that in one class she is to be "taught" by one of the distinguished professors she read about in the university's publicity. The student soon learns that the professor's outstanding reputation was gained because of her research, not her teaching. The professor comes to each class meeting, lectures from yellowed notes, then disappears back into her research, not to be seen by undergraduates until the next lecture.

The lecture method is about as old as the leech treatment, and often just about as effective. Why has it survived? Future professors in their doctoral programs become expert in a narrow segment of a subject area and in research. Rarely are they given any preparation for teaching.

In these two illustrations the hospital was grossly ineffective in meeting the patients' medical needs, as the university was grossly ineffective in meeting students' education needs.

And what if you were not only charged an exorbitant fee for the grossly ineffective medical "service" you received from the hospital, but also a major portion of your fee was used to support the cancer research center, from which you received no direct benefit whatsoever.

Similarly, the university charges undergraduates outrageously high tuition for its half-hearted, very poor educational efforts, and much of the tuition is used to support the graduate school and the university's research programs, from which the undergraduate rarely, if ever, receives any direct benefit.

The hospital promised its patients outstanding health care, which it did not deliver. The university promised its students an excellent education, which it did not deliver.

The hospital's performance would be labeled fraud and malpractice. How would you characterize the university performance?

THE BOOK PLAN

The National Commission on Educating Undergraduates in the Research University (later named the Boyer Commission) was created in 1995 under the auspices of the Carnegie Foundation for the Advancement of Teaching. After three years of exhaustive study, the commission released its report in April 1998. Excerpts from its severe criticisms of undergraduate education in research universities and its recommendations for "widespread and sweeping reform" are presented in chapter 2, along with my comments.

There are 125 research universities among the 3,500 institutions of higher education in America. Chapter 3 will look at the other postsecondary institutions, especially the 1,830 which offer at least a four-year degree, but more importantly, those that offer graduate degrees. Focus will be on those who are attempting to emulate the research universities.

Throughout the remainder of the book, emphasis will be on undergraduate education in research universities and in the 1,830 other universities and colleges that offer at least the bachelor's (four-year) degree.

Chapter 4 looks at serious studies of undergraduate education done earlier in the 1990s and 1980s, whose criticisms are very similar to those of the Boyer Commission. A look at several journalistic pieces on undergraduate education is also provided.

Chapter 5 features a cursory presentation of twenty of the "deadly sins" of universities and colleges, and raises the question: What can be done about the "sins"? Chapters 6 through 14 present eighty radical recommendations for reform.

SPECIAL BULLETIN

In the initial draft of this book, recommendations were made for change in two perceived problem areas.

One concerned fierce, religion-based conflict—Ireland, Bosnia, Israel, and Arabic Muslim countries, even back to the Crusades, etc. The other dealt with the serious financial problems of many universities. Conditions concerning each of those problems have worsened considerably, so now stronger recommendations are being provided.

The horrendous terrorist airliner bombing attacks on the Twin Towers and the Pentagon on September 11, 2001, revealed American vulnerability and changed America forever. The United States subsequently launched military and diplomatic campaigns against the perpetrators of the attacks and their presumed leader Osama bin Laden in Afghanistan.

The United States and its allies must militarily defeat the Taliban in Afghanistan and the al-Qaeda terrorist threats from likely multiple sources. Amicable relations between the United States and the Islamic world are important to each for a number of reasons. So much more than military victories should be pursued.

So far (December 2002) we have done well militarily, but we are losing the public relations war. We need to do a much better job of communicating to the Arab world our goals for a peaceful, fairer world, and, as some experts in Arab cultures have suggested, we need to adopt policies aimed at reversing the sense of humiliation, decline, and despair that sweeps the Arab world.

The role that U.S. universities can play in developing such relations is discussed in Chapter 12 under the heading "Religions."

Second, American higher education has been on a financial roller coaster, especially in the last fifteen years. In the late 1980s and early 1990s, financial conditions of many universities were so desperate that the following options were considered: closing some universities, combining others, eliminating some programs, midyear cuts in already barebones budgets, major cuts in faculty and staff, etc.

In the mid-1990s, an upsurge in the economy enabled many universities to regain financial stability, which lasted about six years.

Now in 2002–2003, universities are again facing serious financial crises, and calls for drastic responses such as the following are being heard:

1. Raising tuition 15 or more percent in consecutive years.
2. Putting a cap on enrollment, denying admission to sizeable numbers of students.
3. Raising admissions requirements, another means to cut student enrollment.
4. Eliminating remedial and other services.
5. Eliminating courses and even programs.

Notice that these and other suggestions being considered would primarily disadvantage students or potential students.

The primary aim of this book is to help college students—especially undergraduates—to really be provided with excellent learning opportunities at reasonable cost.

In this book there are a number of educationally sound cost-cutting suggestions. The following four would serve the students well and be a significant financial boon to the universities and their faculties.

One is Chester Finn's "No Frills University" proposal discussed in chapter 14 under the heading "Rational Radical Reconstructive Reform." If a new university were to be developed, this would be the ideal model. But for many reasons it would seem to be disastrously impossible to graft such a model on an existing university. But some of its useful components, each by itself, could be very valuable additions to an existing institution.

Second is a "fairness in tuition" plan presented in chapter 13 under the heading "Scarlett's Financial Recommendations." The plan would generate considerable additional tuition income for a university, from which could be provided financial assistance to those students who would face severe need because of the change in tuition policy.

Third is a change in faculty responsibilities according to the preference of individual faculty members. This change is discussed in chapter 14 in connection with "Radical Recommendations" 73, 74, 75, and 76. This change would enable each faculty member to concentrate on the major activity of his or her choice. The results will be better teaching, another considerable financial boon for the university, and substantial salary increases for faculty.

Fourth is a strong, campus-wide student retention program discussed in chapter 14 under "Obstacle #27, Indifference to Student Needs." The indefensively high student dropout rate at most universities is at least partially the failure of a university to serve its students well—to put forth a maximum effort to help its students succeed at the institution. A very successful retention program at an institution could be positively life-changing for thousands of students, and also, again, a financial boon to the university.

THE TWO FACES OF AMERICAN HIGHER EDUCATION

Prestigious and knowledgeable observers have said that the United States system of higher education is "the most advanced in the world," "the envy of the world," and "the most effective system of higher education the world has every known." Addressing the Delaware Legislature in May of 1998, then President Clinton said, as he had many times before, "We have the best system of higher education in the world."

High praise, indeed. However, these evaluations are based primarily on the "glamour areas"—research, professional schools, and graduate schools—which, evidence indicates, do deserve a lofty rating.

But it ignores the vast wasteland of neglect and malpractice that is much of American undergraduate education—"education" that fails to provide adequate preparation for vocation and for life to the vast majority of students who enroll as freshmen.

This book will relentlessly scrutinize undergraduate education and other factors affecting it with the intent to uncover all its significant faults, so that a plan of corrective action can be developed. In the process, studies and recommendations of a number of knowledgeable and prestigious groups and individuals will be utilized.

The goal: to raise the level of performance of American undergraduate education to at least the high level of American research, graduate schools, and professional schools.

TWO

CHARACTERIZING THE "RIP-OFF"

THE BOYER COMMISSION REPORT

T he president, Congress, governors, and state legislators seem to be showing little or no apparent concern about the quality of higher education. This is a serious oversight, considering the strong criticism of American higher education—primarily undergraduate education—in a report from the Carnegie Foundation for the Advancement of Teaching issued in April of 1998.

The National Commission on Educating Undergraduates in the Research University was created in 1995 under the auspices of the Carnegie Foundation for the Advancement of Teaching. Later named the Boyer Commission, it submitted its report under the heading, "Reinventing Undergraduate Education: A Blueprint for America's Research Universities."

The report reveals what would seem to be the biggest "rip-off" in American education, and possibly even in American society! The following brief summary of the criticisms in the Boyer Commission report should be helpful in evaluating the "rip-off" charge.

Recruitment materials for undergraduates feature glowing descriptions of world-famous scholars, exciting research in splendid facilities, and the excellence of the education provided. When the students get to the campus, they find that they rarely see "world-famous" scholars, except possibly in a very large (several hundred to one thousand or more students) lecture class; and they have little or no contact with exciting research projects.

As for an "excellent education," what most find is exactly the opposite. The first priority of the university is research, and in the campus reward systems, decisions about tenure, promotion, and salary are based primarily, if not entirely, on the quality and quantity of a faculty member's research. Consequently, faculty are likely to give major emphasis and most of their time to their research—to the detriment of their teaching of undergraduates. The predominate teaching method used is still the lecture, in which the student is a passive listener. This in spite of what research shows: students learn much better when they are active participants in the learning process.

Much of the teaching of undergraduates, especially in the early years, is done by graduate assistants who usually have little if any teaching experience, and whose primary concerns are their own graduate programs, which they are pursuing concurrently with their teaching responsibilities. It's not surprising that emphasis on their studies would sometimes cause them to neglect their teaching responsibilities.

Finally, how could undergraduates be expected to get an "excellent education" when the professors' Ph.D. programs provide expertise in ever-narrowing subject areas and highly developed research skills, but rarely any preparation for teaching?

So undergraduates pay very high tuition costs for a poor education, which the university had led them to believe would be much better. And since the tuition paid by undergraduates is a major source of the research university's income, undergraduates' tuition helps pay the costs of the graduate and research programs, from which the undergraduate usually receives little or no direct benefit!

Is that a "rip-off," or what? The term "rip-off" is not used in the Boyer Commission report, but the criticisms presented there would seem to justify the use of the term.

An examination of the following additional criticisms presented in the commission's own language should further strengthen the case for a "rip-off."

Among its general criticisms, the Boyer Commission report states

the research universities have too often failed, and continue to fail their undergraduate populations. . . . The students paying the tuition get, in all too many cases, less than their money's worth. . . . Again and again, [research] universities are guilty of an advertising practice they would condemn in the commercial world. Recruitment materials display proudly the world-famous professors, the splendid facilities and the ground-breaking research that goes on within them, but thousands of students graduate without ever seeing the world-famous professors or tasting genuine research. Some of their instructors are likely to be badly trained or even untrained teaching assistants who are groping their way toward a teaching technique; some others may be tenured drones who deliver set lectures from yellowed notes, making no effort to engage the bored minds of the students in front of them.

Traditional lecturing should not be the dominant mode of instruction in a research university. . . . The experience of most undergraduates at most research universities is receiving what is served out to them. In one course after another they listen, transcribe, absorb, and repeat, as undergraduates have done for centuries.

Ironically, the first year of university studies, in many ways the most formative of all years, is usually the least satisfactory. . . . Too often the freshman curriculum is a bore and freshman instruction is inadequate.

Senior professors, when they do teach undergraduates, tend to teach majors in advanced courses [where students have likely achieved some competence in learning]. . . . As a result, freshmen—the students who need the very best teaching—may actually receive the worst, and more of them fall away by the end of the freshman year than at any other time.

Many students graduate having accumulated whatever number of courses is required, but still lacking a coherent body of knowledge or any inkling as to how one sort of information might relate to others. All too often they graduate without knowing how to think logically, write clearly, or speak coherently. The university has given them too little that will be of real value beyond a credential that will (may) help them get their first jobs.

Research, according to the Boyer Commission, is the primary mission and concern of the research university; graduate students are a secondary concern; and teaching undergraduates is "a burden shouldered reluctantly to maintain the viability of the institution."

As the Boyer Commission report shows, the primacy of research is everywhere evident: "The standing of a university is measured by the research productivity of its faculty; the place of a department within the university is determined by whether its members garner more or fewer research dollars (grants) and publish more or less noteworthy research than other departments; the stature of the individual within the department is judged by the quantity and quality of the scholarship produced."

Reaffirming the primacy of research in the reward system for faculty, decisions about tenure, promotion, and salary are based primarily on the quantity and quality of a faculty member's research and publication.

The teaching of undergraduates does not receive the best efforts of the university, and is often woefully inadequate. And often the student not only pays the high cost of a poor education, but "tuition income from undergraduates is one of the major sources of university income, helping support research programs and graduate education."

A "rip-off"?

The primary focus of the Boyer Commission report is on improving undergraduate education in the research university, but as part of that process it is necessary to look at the graduate school to see how future college faculty who will teach undergraduates are prepared.

The commision found that "Graduate students are given intensive work in narrowly defined subjects and meticulous training in the technical skills required for research projects"; it is assumed that teaching skills will develop without organized effort. "For many people, that assumption is unwarranted."

A contributing factor to unsatisfactory undergraduate education, then, is that, in doctoral programs, attention is seldom given to the development of teaching and other skills future faculty members will need.

Summing up the criticisms of undergraduate education from the Boyer Commission's report, two quotations stand out. First, "The research universities possess unparalleled wealth in intellectual power and resources; their challenge is to make their baccalaureate students sharers of the wealth. To realize their potential means complete transformation in the nature of the education offered." Second, "We believe that the state of undergraduate education at research universities is such a crisis, an issue of such magnitude and volatility that universities must galvanize themselves to respond." And they must respond now!

LEADERSHIP'S DILEMMA EXPLAINED

It is very easy to understand how many national and state officials and other respected leaders could subscribe to the statement that the United States has the best system of higher education in the world. More than 50 percent of U.S. highschool graduates go on to some kind of college or university experience, a larger percentage than that of any other country in the world. The magnificent research done in U.S. universities has saved and enriched the lives of countless people in the United States and around the world. New surgical and other medical techniques developed in university hospitals have similarly benefited people worldwide.

Graduate schools' faculties have among them the leaders and principal experts in their fields of specialization who have authored the definitive and authoritative books in their fields.

Our graduate schools and professional schools—medical, engineering, business, law, etc.—are "revered" around the globe, attested to by the fact that the best and the brightest students from countries everywhere vie for admission into these schools.

Knowing about these well-publicized successes, it is easy to conclude that U.S. universities are the best in the world, and to assure that everything they do is "world class."

The well-developed criticisms of undergraduate education in research universities presented in the Boyer Commission report presents a compelling case to the contrary. American undergraduate education is presented as far short of "world class"—rather, in fact, badly in need of complete overhaul.

Most of the commission's criticisms are not new. Other prestigious and well-qualified groups and individuals have done intensive studies and leveled the same and additional severe criticisms at undergraduate education over several decades and more. Most of these reports have been written in academic language for academics, although there have been instances where some of the criticisms have been prepared for the general public and presented on television and in general magazines.

Examples of both types of criticism will be presented and discussed in chapter 4.

National and state officials and other leaders who care about the quality of education and the future of America need not feel embarrassed because they were unaware of the severity of the problems of undergraduate education.

But if they are caring leaders, they will realize that, as leaders, they have a responsibility to carefully review the Boyer Commission report, and also check out the reports presented in chapter 4 and others throughout the book, as well as the analysis and recommendations of the author of this book.

The general public needs guidance about higher education. In 1995, studies about what the public thinks about American higher education institutions were conducted for the California Higher Education Policy Center and the American Council on Education. The studies concluded that, lacking knowledge about colleges and universities, the general public has few complaints about higher education. So public pressure has not, in any significant amount, been brought to bear on higher education to undertake reform.

Ironically, if those who have been primarily concerned about the quality of K–12 now turn their attention to the severe criticisms of higher education, they might find help for K–12.

After all, universities and colleges prepare virtually all the teachers and administrators for K–12. If the undergraduate education for those who will teach K–12 students were vastly improved—if, for example, communications skills of the future teachers were greatly improved—doesn't it seem likely that there would be a "trickle-down effect," that the teachers and administrators would be better prepared and therefore able to do a better job of educating K–12 students?

BEYOND THE CRITICISM

To be fair, it must be pointed out that the criticisms of undergraduate education presented do not in their entirety represent the totality of undergraduate education in research universities. But too many are valid for too many institutions.

There are vast differences among research universities. Some do a better job of teaching undergraduates than others do. Some professors within an institution do a better job than their colleagues.

Some undergraduates at research universities get an excellent education, but it seems likely this success would be in spite of the system, rather than because of it.

The Boyer Commission report not only points out the weaknesses in undergraduate programs, but also recommends a meticulously and very thoughtfully crafted plan to rectify problems they see at research universities.

REINVENTING UNDERGRADUATE EDUCATION

There has been some recognition in research universities in recent years of the need to improve the education of their undergraduates, but as the Boyer Commission's report notes, they "have opted for cosmetic surgery, taking a nip here and a tuck there, when radical reconstruction is called for. . . . Too often bold and promising efforts have vanished after external grant support disappeared."

In research universities their research missions are valued above all else, according to the Boyer Commission report, but undergraduates are generally not participants in that mission. Rather, most are taught by telling—the transmission of information through lecturing.

Inquiry-based learning is recommended instead of the usual lecture method. According to the Boyer Commission report, "The basic idea of learning as inquiry is the same as research; even though advanced research occurs at advanced levels, undergraduates beginning in the freshman year can learn through research. . . . [I]n a setting in which inquiry is prized, every course in an undergraduate curriculum should provide an opportunity for a student to succeed through discovery-based methods."

The new model of undergraduate education being proposed in the Boyer Commission report makes the baccalaureate experience an inseparable part of an integrated whole—research-inquiry centered. "Everyone at a (research) university should be a discoverer, a learner. . . . [T]he skills of analysis, evaluation, and synthesis will become the hallmarks of a good education, just as the absorption of a body of knowledge once was."

As outlined in the Boyer Commission report, some components of a "new model" would be:

"The goal of making baccalaureate [undergraduate] students partici-pants in the research process requires faculties to reexamine their methods of delivering education, to ask how, in every course, students can become active rather than passive learners. That task undertaken seriously will produce many innovations suited to different disciplinary circumstances; the changes need to include greater expectations of writing and speaking, more active problem solving, and greater collaborating among baccalau-reate students, graduate students, and faculty."

Long-term mentoring is an important aspect of the plan:

> Every student at a research university should be able to feel that some faculty member knows and appreciates that student's situation and progress and is ready to help that progress by setting standards to be met and by offering advice, encouragement, and criticism. . . . This kind of a mentoring relationship needs to be created early and maintained throughout a student's program.
>
> Thoughtful advising and mentoring should integrate major fields with supporting courses so that programs become integrated wholes rather than collections of disparate courses.
>
> The focal point of the freshman year should be a small seminar taught by experienced faculty. The seminar should deal with topics that will stimulate and open intellectual horizons and allow opportunities for learning by inquiry in a collaborative environment. Working in small groups will give students not only direct intellectual contact with fac-ulty and with one another, but also give those new to their situations opportunities to find friends and to learn how to be students.
>
> The freshman program should be carefully constructed as an inte-grated interdisciplinary, inquiry-based experience by designs such as: combining a group of students with a combination of faculty and grad-uate assistants for a semester or a year of study of a single complicated subject or problem.
>
> The failure of research universities seems most serious in conferring degrees upon inarticulate students. . . . Dissemination of results is an essential and integral part of the research process.

The development of written and oral communications skills should be emphasized in every course.

Technology, another important aspect of the Boyer Commision's plan, can greatly enhance student learning. Faculty need to think carefully "not only how to make the most effective use of existing technologies but also how to create new ones that will enhance their own teaching and that of their colleagues. The best teachers and researchers should be thinking about how to design courses in which technology enriches teaching rather than substitutes for it."

The reexamination and restructuring of undergraduate education, as per the Boyer Commission report in 1998 and the other recommendations of expert individuals and groups over the past several decades, must make the study of educational technology a major focus. A discussion of educational technology *with special emphasis on the Internet* is provided in chapter 11 under the heading "Fantastic Fantasy Future."

The practical experience of internships "can offer an invaluable adjunct to research-based learning by allowing the student concrete contexts in which to apply research principles." Instead of completing the senior year with just the addition of some more courses, a capstone experience is strongly recommended. As the Boyer Commission report notes, "All the skills of research developed in earlier work should be marshaled in a project that demands the framing of a significant question or set of questions, the research or creative exploration to find answers, and the communication skills to convey the results to audiences both expert and uninitiated in the subject matter."

Before such a "new model" of undergraduate education can be implemented, it will be necessary for the reward system for faculty to be completely overhauled. Faculty will need to know that tenure, promotion, and salary decisions will be based equally on evaluation of their teaching performance as well as their research performance. And salary for top teaching should be able to reach the same level as salary for top research.

COMMENTS ABOUT THE NEW MODEL

The proposed new model would make the undergraduate experience an inseparable part of an integrated whole university that is research-inquiry centered. Long-term mentoring for each student by a faculty member would be an important component, as would a small seminar for freshmen. An excellent feature would be the integrated interdisciplinary, inquiry-based experience combining a group of students with a combination of faculty and graduate assistants for a semester or a year of study of a single complicated subject or problem. Developing student communications skills in each course is very commendable, as is the capstone experience.

These and the other recommendations seem theoretically very sound, but implementation would almost surely present seemingly insurmountable problems. All will require faculty to give much more time to undergraduates, time they will have to take from their research on the cutting edge of the fragment of their discipline specialization.

Students complain that a great many faculty are not available to sign their registration slips, let alone advise them, but are off working on research. Graduate students and part-time faculty do much of the teaching of undergrads, so that faculty can spend more time on their advanced research projects.

Large freshman classes—sometimes enrolling as many as one thousand students—are provided so that one professor can do the job of about thirty professors teaching reasonably sized classes. This again frees much more professors' time for advanced research.

The recommended greatly increased time professors would spend with undergraduates would greatly reduce the time professors would be able to spend on "cutting-edge" research.

Or, universities could hire many more professors to help divide up the considerable extra time to be spent with undergraduates. This, of course, would greatly increase the expenses of the universities, which they must not pass on to students through increases in tuition, which is already outrageously high at many universities.

The cost factor and motivating highly research-oriented faculty to spend much more time with undergraduates are two of the most challenging hurdles which must be overcome if the Boyer Commission's recommended new model of undergraduate education is to become a reality in research universities.

WHAT IS A RESEARCH UNIVERSITY?

Contributing to the problems of individualizing undergraduate education is the fact that many research universities have very large undergraduate enrollments. While research universities make up only 3 percent of the total number of American institutions of higher learning, they confer 32 percent of the baccalaureate—generally four-year—degrees.

In 1994, the Carnegie Foundation identified 125 institutions as research universities in two categories:

Eighty-eight "Research I" universities "offer a full range of baccalaureate programs, are committed to graduate education through the doctorate, and give high priority to research. They award fifty or more doctoral degrees each year. In addition they receive annually $40 million or more in federal support."

An additional thirty-seven institutions are called "Research II" universities; they receive between $15.5 million and $40 million in federal support, but are otherwise like the Research I universities.

As I explain throughout this book, the concern is about undergraduate education in virtually all colleges and universities offering at least four-year degrees—bachelor's degrees. Almost all the other studies and recommendations that will be referred to have been done about the wide range of four-year institutions. But there is commonality not only among the earlier studies, but also between them and the Boyer Commission report.

A number of the Boyer Commission recommendations designed for the research universities could be helpful to virtually all four-year institutions.

Also, the Boyer Commission explains that its concern is primarily with "how subject matter is presented and how intellectual growth is stimulated" in research universities. While this concern is central and of great importance, there are other factors that can have a major impact on the effectiveness or lack of effectiveness of undergraduate education: the campus environment, the academic program, who the students are, governance, leadership, internal management, and costs to students.

The next chapter will look at the complexity of the American structure of higher education and identify its various components.

THREE
HOMOGENIZATION

C hapter 2 dealt with undergraduate education in the 125 American research universities, which make up only 3 percent of the roughly thirty-five hundred higher education institutions in the country. This chapter will briefly examine some of the types of institutions that make up the other 97 percent, and how they relate to the research universities.

About 1,545 colleges offer no work beyond associate (two-year) degree programs. There are 526 private two-year colleges, and 1,019 community colleges.

Community colleges began to appear early in the twentieth century, and it was the explosive growth of these colleges in the mid- and late twentieth century that is largely responsible for the phenomenal, unparalleled proportion of Americans afforded postsecondary educational opportunity. By the 1980s community colleges operated in every state and enrolled half the students who began college in America.

Among those served by community colleges were those whose prior academic records prevented them from gaining admission to four-year colleges and universities, and remedial work was provided for these students.

Community colleges were generally placed in or near population centers, so that with no, or very low tuition, and no room and board costs (since students could drive to the not-too-distant campuses), the financially deprived could attend college.

Thus, vast numbers of people with academic or financial deficiencies who otherwise would not have been able to attend college were now added to the college population through the community colleges.

Community college also catered to persons with full-time jobs, making complete programs available to them at night or on weekends; and individual courses were provided in virtually any subject the people in the community wished to study.

Students can take freshman and sophomore courses, which can be transferred toward a bachelor's degree in a four-year college or university, or they can earn a two-year terminal (associate) degree in vocational-technical education, or they can complete a program of training for a specific occupation in less than two years, or simply take individual courses that interest them.

There is no confusion about the mission of the two-year institution. It is teaching. If occasionally a teacher wishes to do some research, it is likely this would be permitted if it does not interfere with or detract from a faculty member's teaching and related activities.

There are about 455 colleges whose highest degree offered is the bachelor's degree. Like community colleges, such institutions might be expected to resist emulating the research and publication. But, "it ain't necessarily so."

Among this group of institutions are liberal arts colleges whose concern has, over the years, been the providing of a "well-rounded" education, even the development of the "whole student."

But even in these four-year institutions whose traditional role has been teaching, there has been evidence that the assertion that "research is the cornerstone of higher education" is gaining greater acceptance. More faculty members are doing research and publishing scholarly articles and books. As long as this activity does not diminish the teaching role, it can be a very positive development.

However, some liberal arts colleges have gone further. Roger Bowen illustrated this trend in an article in the *Chronicle of Higher Education.*

Bowen says that when he was hired at Colby College (Maine) in 1978, Colby was considered a top liberal arts college in the traditional sense. While some publishing was done, the primary commitment was to teaching. But Bowen explains that sometime later

> . . . a system was introduced that made explicit the need for faculty
> members to publish if they wanted to advance their careers; tenure, pro-
> motion, and salary increases came to depend more and more on pub-

lishing. Faculty members' teaching loads were reduced from six courses a year to five, partly as an inducement to [do research and] publish. Today, the likelihood of being tenured without at least one book (or an equivalent number of articles) to one's credit is minimal. . . . Excellence in teaching falls behind publication in determining merit pay. . . . A consequence of de-emphasis on teaching has been that tenure and other rewards have been given to good scholars who are not effective teachers and denied to excellent teachers with only mildly impressive scholarly records.

Colby has demeaned one of the most important qualities that define a small liberal-arts college—a faculty committed primarily to teaching—by forcibly recasting its faculty in the image of those at large research institutions.

Of the thirty-five hundred higher education institutions in the United States, the 125 research universities were examined in Chapter 1; the 1,545 two-year colleges, and the 455 whose highest degree offered is the bachelor's degree—a four-year degree—have been discussed; now the remaining 1,375 institutions will be reviewed.

All of the 1,375 have graduate programs, some offering only the master's degree, some offering doctoral programs that produce a relatively few doctoral graduates a year; others produce a large number of doctoral graduates, although fewer than the fifty of the research universities, and they receive less than $15.5 million in federal support per year.

Among this group are former liberal arts colleges that have broadened their undergraduate programs, added graduate programs, and increased their research commitment.

Another relatively large segment consider themselves "institutions in transition," best illustrated by state-established two-year normal schools for the preparation of public school teachers, later expanded into four-year teachers' colleges, some next designated as regional universities, and a still-smaller number authorized by their state legislature as comprehensive universities.

These institutions also have increased their number of undergraduate programs, developed more graduate programs, and increased their research commitments.

All of this development is not coincidental, and it has been going on for some time. *Reform on Campus*, a 1972 Carnegie report on the status of U.S. higher education, described what it called a rapidly developing *homogenization*—institutions becoming more and more alike.

And in 1987 in *College*—the report on Carnegie's exhaustive three-year higher education study—Ernest Boyer indicated that there was a strong and growing movement among America's diverse institutions to emulate the prestige institutions—the research universities. Thus as they patterned themselves after research universities, American colleges and universities were becoming more and more homogeneous.

A great many institutions changed the emphasis in their reward systems from teaching to research, and they assigned large numbers of inexperienced graduate students and part-time teachers to teach undergraduates.

And individual professors on a great many campuses, whether the institution emphasis was on research or not, sought recognition through research and publication in their area of specialization rather than through effective teaching.

This elitist, prestige-driven movement has continued at an ever more rapid pace, which means that what seemed so alarming in chapter 1—the very poor undergraduate education offered in many of the 125 research universities—was only the tip of the iceberg. It seems very likely that considerably more than one thousand institutions are caught up to a greater or lesser degree in the homogenization movement.

What this adds up to is that a very great number of undergraduates are being ripped off, and that undergraduate education is in serious trouble —probably more serious than K–12's troubles.

Those concerned about K–12 are still looking for answers. Some answers for undergraduate reform might come through the homogenization which has been deplored in this book as the major cause of the widespread deterioration of undergraduate education.

If the Boyer Commission's plan for the rejuvenation of undergraduate education in research universities can actually be implemented, and nonresearch institutions still pattern themselves after research universities, then a widespread renaissance of undergraduate education can be confidently predicted. For example, just look at one statement from the commission's report: "The goal of making baccalaureate students participate in the research process requires faculties to reexamine their methods of delivering education, to ask how, in every course, students can become active rather than passive learners." Some institutions may not have the inclination or the capability to involve the students in the "research process," but if learning is substituted for research in the above quote, it then becomes a significant guideline for the improvement of any undergraduate program.

Among other recommendations from the Commission that could be very helpful to any four-year institution are: the freshman seminar, oral and written communication skills emphasis, inquiry-based courses, use of educational technology, internships, mentoring, interdisciplinary courses studying a complicated subject or problem, the capstone experience, the preparation in graduate school of future college teachers for teaching, and alteration of the reward system.

WHEN AND HOW DID IT BEGIN?

The research emphasis versus the teaching emphasis is at the heart of the deterioration of undergraduate education in America.

Distinguished educator Abraham Flexner put it graphically when at a higher-education meeting in Chicago in 1905 he said ". . . the university has sacrificed college teaching at the altar of research."

How has this come about? A brief look backward should provide some insights.

America's first higher education institutions were based on the English model, whose emphasis was on educating the student.

During the nineteenth century, thousands of American students went to Germany and earned Ph.D. degrees, which emphasized research and the advancement of the disciplines—areas of specialization. Many of the Americans with German Ph.D.s came home and joined college faculties, which brought about the development of American graduate schools.

Thus an incongruous situation developed in which the German model graduate school devoted to research and advancement of the discipline was placed atop the English model undergraduate school whose concern was educating undergraduates.

And the graduate schools began "preparing" the faculty for undergraduate schools. What the graduate schools' faculty did was clone themselves in their Ph.D. programs, instead of providing their students with what they would need to be effective teachers of undergraduates.

The Boyer Commission's expressed concerns are particularly about undergraduate education in the 125 research universities.

American universities' magnificent accomplishments in research and scholarship must not be diminished, but ways must be found to achieve the same level of achievement in undergraduate education.

FOUR

DECADES OF CRITICISM, BUSINESS AS USUAL

Once again it should be pointed out that America's national and state political leaders and other leaders such as consumer advocate Ralph Nader have been almost uniformly silent about the severe neglect and mistreatment of thousands and thousands of undergraduates (consumers) in many of America's universities and colleges.

Of course these leaders face many serious, urgent, and often very complex problems at home and abroad that demand their attention. And granted, the outstanding achievements of many universities in some endeavors can understandably blind noneducators to the dismal performance in much of undergraduate education.

Also, as we have noted already, studies that over the years have been very critical of higher education (a few of which will be encapsulated later in this chapter) have usually been prepared for academics and primarily circulated among them.

But in recent years there have been a few very revealing pieces on higher education prepared in journalistic styles and placed in the popular media for the general public. Examples are the March 17, 1997, *Time* magazine cover story, "How Colleges Are Gouging You: A Special Investigation into Why Tuition Has Soared"; a *60 Minutes* segment; and a Delta *Sky* magazine story. Excerpts from the latter two follow.

It is surprising that the aforementioned leaders' staffs apparently didn't alert their bosses to these pieces and even look further into each.

THE EXPOSÉ

On February 26, 1995, cohost Lesley Stahl of *60 Minutes* presented a program segment that revealed shocking information about American undergraduate education to the general public. Here are some excerpts from the program:

As the camera pans over a class in session at the University of Arizona, in a voice-over Ms. Stahl says, "Can you find the professor in this picture? No, because the teacher of this English composition class is a graduate student. It's the same story in the 149 other freshman English classes; not a single professor at Arizona teaches freshman English."

Stahl continues the voice-over, this time while the camera pans a calculus class: "You would see the same thing at universities all across the country. The only time most freshmen see real professors is in huge lecture classes. At the University of Arizona, freshmen are taught by grad students or part-timers 87 percent of the time. Most . . . have little or no training as teachers. And what's worse, in the sciences, some can barely speak English."

Professor Dennis Huston of Rice University affirms, "That's true. . . . It happens everywhere in major universities."

Professor Huston is an English professor at Rice University, who a few years ago was selected as the best college teacher in America.

Commenting on the college teaching profession, Huston says, ". . . if you are absolutely successful, you are promoted out of the possibility of having to teach. What universities are looking for are people who do what is conceived to be important research. . . . They write books which are noticed in the press. And, in fact, there's a kind of contempt that goes with teaching undergraduates sometimes because it gets in the way of their published research."

While the camera focuses on Professor Solomon, who teaches classics at Arizona, Ms. Stahl points out in a voice-over, John Solomon says, "aspiring scholars get an unmistakable message: teaching doesn't count."

Professor Solomon then elaborates: "One's time is spent, one's energies are spent, one's hopes and dreams are spent on the publications and not on the teaching. I've heard stories of young teachers being told, 'You're a very good teacher. The students tell me you're a good teacher.

Obviously, you're spending too much time on your teaching. You'd better spend more time on your publications.'"

Ms. Stahl in voice-over: "Spend more time on your publications or you won't get tenure, the lifetime job guarantee that universities give their faculties. . . . You're absolutely telling me . . . that teaching doesn't mean anything to get tenure?"

And further, Solomon says: "As a tenured professor at any university, teaching means very little."

Hanson adds: ". . . tenured professors have no motivation to be good teachers. So . . . it's the attitude of, 'I have other things to do. I have research to do. I have papers to write.'"

Ms. Stahl in voice-over: "Right there, in the University of Arizona tenure guidelines, it tells every candidate to count up all the pages in all of the articles they've published . . . because professors seeking tenure must publish or perish, an entire industry exists just to give them places to publish, so-called scholarly journals. The University of Arizona spends more than $4 million a year subscribing to 20,000 journals, [for example,] 45 different journals on entomology, the study of bugs. And, let's be honest. Nobody reads them."

Professor Huston: "Very few people, right—three or four friends or three or four people in the same field."

Ms. Stahl: "Now, I can just see parents out there listening to what you're saying and thinking, 'I'm forking out $15,000 to $20,000 now—and that's what it costs—to send my kid to a school where what I'm doing is subsidizing some guy's research. I thought I was forking out this money to educate my kids.'"

Professor Huston: "I think it's important that the customer know that the customer is not always getting what the customer thinks he's getting."

Professor Soloman: "I'm waiting for some powerful parent to sue a university for consumer fraud. You're paying this money, you're trying to get a product, and you're not getting it."

An article by journalist and part-time college instructor Timothy Harper in the October 1995 issue of *Sky* magazine gives a specific example of the lack of concern for its undergraduates exhibited by many universities.

> Richard Barr, Ph.D., is a remarkably gifted, effective, and committed professor [at Rutgers University]. He is also about to lose his job

because he spends too much time on his students and not enough on research to produce scholarly articles that almost no one would read. The case of Rick Barr, and many other professors committed to their students, reads as a sad comment on priorities in American higher education . . . the university's tenure committee believes Barr has not done enough pure academic research to receive tenure—a permanent position with virtual career-long job security. So Barr is in effect being fired [after nearly nine years at Rutgers].

Harper explains that many major universities don't want faculty who are good teachers; they want faculty who are good researchers. This accounts for the fact that although professors are the teachers of record, particularly of introductory courses for freshmen, often the professor is off doing research while "the actual lecturing—and grading—is handled by nameless faces, young grad-school teaching assistants who have little teaching experience or training. . . ."

According to Harper, "Barr works 70-plus hours a week." He supervises student groups, and "while many professors duck office hours . . . Barr strongly encourages his students to make regular visits."

Barr has won teaching awards from faculty, student, and parent groups. His colleagues in the English department voted forty to five in favor of granting him tenure. Harper quotes two evaluations in his article. The first, an evaluation from a superior in the English department, said: "Few junior faculty members have had such direct and sustained influence on undergraduate education at Rutgers as Richard Barr."

The second, a student evaluation, said: "His love for his work and his devotion to his students is inspirational. His enthusiasm and his motivation are contagious and make students really want to learn and understand."

But Rutgers students will be deprived of his services.

Admittedly, *60 Minutes* looks for sensational, often shocking stories, but it has the reputation for doing good, hard-hitting, accurate reporting.

Though *Sky*, published by Delta Airlines, is a rather obscure general interest magazine, it is usually of high quality. Timothy Harper is a journalist who has taught part-time at several universities.

Neither of the two media provided intensive study and long-time observation by its staff, but they did accurately portray what's happening on many university campuses.

And what they showed is only the tip of the iceberg, as examination of many thorough studies throughout this book will show.

STUDY CAPSULES

Because of the snail's pace of change in higher education, studies, analyses, and recommendations of ten, fifteen, or even more years ago often have unchanged relevance for today.

For example, among the studies of the mid-1980s are a federally sponsored study by the National Institute of Education (NIE); a study by the American Association of Colleges (AAC), a national organization of educators; the Carnegie study, sponsored by a private foundation; a study of a special state commission in California; and a study by the National Endowment for the Humanities (NEH).

There is surprising commonality in the reports of these diverse groups, as indicated by this comment in the AAC report: "When our committee was formed, . . . we feared that our eventual report would be a voice crying in the wilderness. We now know that we have joined a chorus." The following excerpts from various reports illustrate the point:

- The NIE report says the quality of undergraduate education is in decline. "The realities of student learning, curricular coherence, . . . and academic standards no longer measure up to our expectations. . . . The gaps between the ideal and the actual are serious warning signals."
- The AAC report says "there is a profound crisis" in undergraduate education. "Evidence of decline and devaluation is everywhere. . . . The bachelor's degree has become a virtually meaningless credential."
- The mid-1980s Carnegie study says that the undergraduate college "is a troubled institution" and that "undergraduate colleges in the United States are confused over their purposes and racked by tensions that prevent them from providing coherent educational experiences."
- The NEH report called for a restoration of coherence and vitality to undergraduate programs in the humanities.
- The California legislative panel received a barrage of criticism about the quality of teaching on university campuses, along with

criticism that undergraduates were being virtually ignored by their professors, who allegedly were more concerned about research.

In its mid-1980s study, the AAC goes to the heart of what has been happening to undergraduate education as follows: ". . . the development that overwhelmed the old curriculum and changed the entire nature of higher education was the transformation of the professors from teachers concerned with the characters and minds of their students to professionals, scholars with Ph.D. degrees with an allegiance to academic disciplines stronger than their commitment to teaching, or to the life of the institutions where they are employed."

The fact that the faults in undergraduate education identified in the AAC and other studies in the mid-1980s still exist and have even worsened is pointed out in the *60 Minutes* segment more than a decade later.

Also, in their well-researched 1995 book, *The Abandoned Generation: Rethinking Higher Education*, Professors William Willimon and Thomas Naylor take an even tougher stand on the professorate, reinforcing charges leveled in the *60 Minutes* report as follows: "We use the students to *finance* our writing and research, as a base from which to promote ourselves within our professional guilds and disciplines, but we do not really engage them in education."

PROF-SCAM

One of the most excoriating criticisms of professors in higher education was presented in 1988 by Charles J. Sykes in his book, *ProfScam: Professors and the Demise of Higher Education*.

Sykes attacks university professors

> . . . for being overpaid and "grotesquely underworked," neglecting their students to work on meaningless research, turning their classes over to incompetent teaching assistants, distorting the curriculum to pursue narrow and selfish interests, speaking in pompous "prof-speak," and using their unique system of academic freedom and tenure to protect behavior that would be inexcusable anywhere else.
>
> Almost single-handedly, the professors . . . have destroyed the uni-

versity as a center of learning. Professors have convinced society that this [academic] culture is essential for higher learning, and thus have been able to protect their own status and independence while cheating students, parents, taxpayers and employers and polluting the intellectual inheritance of society.

A former journalist and professor, Sykes's book may represent the sensationalism often attributed to journalists, but there is much truth and some wisdom in the book.

(It is important to note that in this book—the RIP-OFF—the villain is "the system," not the faculty, the administration, or the governing board.)

The report of another significant study of primarily undergraduate education was distributed in January of 1994. Titled *An American Imperative: Higher Expectations for Higher Education*, the report was prepared by the Wingspread Group of 16 who had been assembled by four foundations to examine the question: What does society need from higher education? Thirty-two distinguished and knowledgeable essayists wrote on the question to augment the input of the Group of 16.

As it looked at a changing America in a changing world, the group concluded that "a dangerous mismatch exists between what American society needs of higher education and what it is receiving," and that "society must hold higher education to much higher expectations or risk national decline."

The group calls for the regeneration of undergraduate education institution by institution, which "will require rethinking the assumptions of the education enterprise and reinventing many of its ways of doing business."

The focus of the report is on the decline of undergraduate education, virtually the same focus as the NIE, AAC, Carnegie, and NEH studies of the mid-1980s, but in addition the Wingspread Group put strong emphasis on the need for values education and the need to contain the wildly escalating costs to students.

Twenty-two of the Wingspread essayists strongly recommended emphasis on values. This is in harmony with the bemoaned decline of values in society in recent years, and even worse than the decline, in the eyes of some writers, is that a great many Americans don't seem to care about it.

To illustrate, some have pointed to former President Clinton and Newt Gingrich.

On election day in November 1996, voters were asked if they thought the President was honest; 54 percent said they did not, but they elected him anyway.

In January 1997, Speaker Newt Gingrich of the House of Representatives was reprimanded for ethics violations by an overwhelming (395-28) vote of the House, and fined $300,000. Gingrich was the first speaker of the house to be reprimanded for ethics violations, and the $300,000 penalty is the largest ever assessed on a member of the House. Yet Gingrich was reelected speaker and continued in that role for some time.

The Wingspread Group also sees the rapidly rising costs to students threatening to greatly limit student access to higher education. If the trend of the past fifteen years continues, access is likely to be severely limited.

Note that tuition at public four-year colleges and universities rose 234 percent between 1980–81 and 1994–95, according to a report released in August of 1996 by the General Accounting Office of the U.S. Congress During this same period, median household income rose only 82 percent and the cost of consumer goods rose only 74 percent.

While only brief excerpts have been presented here, they accurately represent the essence of the in-depth studies of undergraduate education, which were staffed by experts, carefully planned, very thoroughly pursued, the findings effectively presented, and astute recommendations for improvement provided. Other equally impressive studies and observations during the 1980s and on through the 1990s combine to provide a vast body of knowledge about the abysmal condition of undergraduate education on a great many campuses, but all of this has had little perceptible effect on the institutions!

WHY THE LACK OF RESPONSE?

Why, in the light of overwhelmingly authoritative analyses and recommendations, have colleges and universities made such minimal positive change?

There are probably a number of reasons, including the following: First, "if it's not broken, don't fix it!" Many in higher education don't see the need for much change. After all, they've got a comfortable situation that favors them.

When administrators encourage faculty research with lightened teaching loads and a reward system based primarily on research productivity, they can make determinations about tenure, promotion, and salary increases by counting the number of books and articles produced by faculty. This method of evaluation is much easier than evaluating teaching and student advising effectiveness, participation on campus committees, and contributions to the development of interdisciplinary courses or campuswide curriculum to meet student needs.

Also, by concentrating on faculty research, administration then finds little need to supervise faculty teaching and related activities, thus avoiding the possibility of conflict with faculty over the interpretation of academic freedom. And they avoid the possibility of having to face litigation because of the current imprecise methods of evaluating teaching and other faculty nonresearch activities.

Faculty, on the other hand, know they are pretty much given a free hand to pursue their own interests—research and distinction in their individual disciplines—while giving minimal attention to teaching and other campus activities, and they will be rewarded for so doing.

Marshall and Tucker say in the Wingspread Report: "Too much of education at every level seems to be organized for the convenience of educators and the institutions' interests, procedures, and prestige, and too little focused on the needs of students." And Frank Newman said in *Choosing Quality*, "Left totally to its own, the university will evolve toward self-interest, rather than public interest." It appears this is what has happened. In a system that so blatantly favors both administrators and faculty, why would they be interested in widespread change?

Second, what is the process for change in colleges and universities? George Keller wrote in *Academic Strategy* in 1983 that *incrementalism* has been and still is the method of change in higher education in 90 percent of the institutions. In incrementalism, change is brought about by a number of tiny little steps, through bargaining that considers people's self-interest and their "territories." Such a system cannot deal with comprehensive, radical change.

Third, the great diversity of America's system of higher education has become increasingly more homogenized over the last few decades, in part because of the desire to emulate the 125 prestigious research universities.

Research universities, in spite of their magnificent accomplishments in research and scholarship and in their graduate and professional schools, often neglect their undergraduate programs, emphasizing research over teaching, the curriculum, and the undergraduate student, as the Boyer Commission indicated.

Most of the recommendations of the studies are aimed at improving undergraduate education, but the "copycat" institutions have set their sights on the perceived prestige research and graduate school development, and pay little attention to the recommendations of the studies.

Fourth, significantly and sadly, most students and their parents have seemed satisfied with credentialing rather than real learning. As long as the students were awarded degrees, they and their parents generally have not evinced much concern about the amount or the content of the learning which led to the receiving of the degrees.

Fifth, the 75 percent of the general public who never graduated from college, including many whose children are now undergraduates, know little about what professors and administrators do, what is taught in classrooms and laboratories, and how colleges and universities conduct their business, according to 1995 studies conducted for the California Higher Education Policy Center and the American Council on Education. The studies conclude that, lacking knowledge about colleges and universities, the general public has few complaints about higher education. So public pressure has not, in any significant amount, been brought to bear on higher education to undertake reform.

Sixth, the studies, so critical of higher education, were prepared primarily for educators, not the general public, often using a complex writing style with higher education jargon sprinkled liberally throughout. Thus, the studies received little attention from the general public, and failed to stimulate public concern.

FIVE

FRAUD IN HIGHER EDUCATION?

Extractions from the beginning of the Wingspread Report were presented in the preceding chapter, but for emphasis on the highly critical nature of the current state of undergraduate education, several complete quotations from the first page of the report will be presented here.

> A disturbing and dangerous mismatch exists between what American society needs of higher education and what it is receiving. Nowhere is the mismatch more dangerous than in the quality of undergraduate preparation provided on many campuses. The American imperative for the twenty-first century is that society must hold higher education to much higher expectations or risk national decline.
>
> Education is in trouble, and with it our nation's hopes for the future. America's ability to compete in a global economy is threatened. The American people's hopes for a civil, humane society ride on the outcome. The capacity of the United States to shoulder its responsibilities on the world stage is at risk.
>
> The simple fact is that some faculties and institutions certify for graduation too many students who cannot read and write very well, too many whose intellectual depth and breadth are unimpressive, and too many whose skills are inadequate in the face of the demands of contemporary life.

If, as seems likely, the Wingspread report and the Boyer Commission report, as did their predecessors, ignite only some sparks and an occasional, flickering flame, what will fan the sparks and flickering flames? What will ignite a raging fire that sweeps across a concerned public and even higher education, generating a heat that can forge a new undergraduate education to serve the futuristic world of the twenty-first century?

Perhaps the following hard-hitting and unvarnished thumbnail description of U.S. four-year undergraduate education will help.

THE TWENTY DEADLY SINS

In their catalogs and promotion materials, a great many colleges and universities present a glowing description of the excellence of education they provide to their undergraduates, but they do not follow through. They seem to show little concern for the education of the undergraduates they enroll.

Consider the following twenty of the "deadly" sins of colleges and universities:

Sin 1: They hire faculty who are unprepared to teach. The Ph.D., the ultimate qualification for a faculty position, is not a teaching degree.

Sin 2: They lack programs to help faculty learn to teach.

Sin 3: They hire department chairpersons without knowledge of teaching or management to "supervise" college teachers and manage departments.

Sin 4: The lecture method, in which the student is a passive listener, is the predominate method of teaching in most universities, even though learning and long-term retention is greatly enhanced when the student is an active participant in the learning process.

Sin 5: Large classes enrolling two hundred to one thousand students are provided during the freshman year, when the student needs personal attention most.

Sin 6: Because of a misinterpretation of academic freedom, administrators play virtually no role in how the faculty teach, what they teach, or whether the faculty ignore the catalog description of the education the institution promised to its students. Academic freedom, as it is now interpreted, permits and protects poor teaching.

Sin 7: Not only are faculty allowed to "do their thing their way," most will be awarded tenure, which is virtually a lifetime contract, without the requirement of initial or continuing excellent or even good performance in teaching.

Sin 8: Ph.D. programs—the predominate and prestige "preparation" for faculty—prepare faculty to be experts in depth in a narrow area of knowledge. Undergraduates need teachers with breadth who can help them integrate knowledge—see the broad picture—and who can develop broad courses to meet student needs instead of more highly specialized courses in which individual faculty have a special interest.

Sin 9: The highly specialized faculty have developed such flexibility in graduation requirements that students can earn degrees by taking many narrowly specialized and seemingly unrelated courses that leave them without a coherent education.

Sin 10: Ph.D. programs prepare future faculty with research skills, which are customarily utilized by faculty in producing research on the fringe of their narrow specialized areas, research that generally has little relevance for their undergraduate students.

Sin 11: Reward systems in a great many colleges and universities place much more emphasis on research and publishing productivity than on teaching effectiveness. The awarding of tenure, promotion, and significant salary increases is primarily based on such "scholarly" productivity.

Sin 12: Faculty at most institutions have been given smaller teaching loads to provide them more time to do research. Lower teaching loads mean more faculty must be hired for the same number of students (a great increase in expenses). So student fees are increased to subsidize research, not teaching.

Sin 13: Additionally, students say faculty are seldom available outside the classroom for advising, counseling, or helping students to learn, but rather are off pursuing their own interests—research, publication, consulting, etc.

Sin 14: Primarily because they cost much less, the proportion of part-time faculty members in the United States has increased to 41 percent. At a typical institution like the University of Arizona, freshmen are taught by graduate students or part-timers 87 percent of the time.

The graduate students are primarily concerned with their own graduate studies, rather than the teaching of their freshman classes.

The part-time teachers are usually busy professionals—noneducators—who dash out to a campus to teach a class, immediately after which they disappear back into their full-time jobs, and are unavailable to students.

Also, retention studies have identified the first six weeks of the freshman year as the most critical time in determining whether students will succeed and persist to the achieving of a four-year degree. During this period and throughout the year, the studies indicate, freshmen need the best and most caring teachers who will stimulate them to learn in class and be available to help them outside of class. The Boyer Commission concurs.

Sin 15: The most damning evidence that some universities care little about their undergraduates is the fact that they assign teaching responsibilities to persons who are unable to communicate effectively in spoken English.

This can occur when a foreign professor is hired because of an outstanding research record, even though students have great difficulty understanding him or her in class. And, since graduate students come to American universities in great numbers from all around the world, many become teaching assistants, especially in the sciences, even though some can barely speak English.

Sin 16: At a great many institutions, a freshman arriving on campus is thrust into a student culture which features widespread partying; binge drinking; sexual promiscuity; date rape, theft, and other crimes; violence; cheating on tests and writing assignments; overemphasis on intercollegiate athletics; and other activities which create an anti-intellectual climate seldom countered by university efforts. Such an environment makes it extremely difficult for beginning students, as well as upperclassmen, to initiate and sustain successful intellectual and academic endeavors.

Sin 17: The first fourteen sins represent gross neglect of undergraduates' academic-intellectual development and skills. Additionally, at a great many universities there is nearly total neglect of the students' personal development—their morals, ethics, values, etc.

Sin 18: Management of the institutions is inefficient, grossly wasting resources. "Organized anarchy" is how many institutions' internal operations have been described.

Sin 19: It should be no surprise, then, that the lack of attention to undergraduate education results in low graduation rates—only about 50 percent of students who enroll as freshmen graduate—and low achievement levels of a great many who do graduate. According to the 1993 National Adult Literacy Survey, surprisingly large numbers of college graduates are unable, in everyday situations, to use basic skills involving reading, writing, computation, and elementary problem-solving.

So, students leave many universities often without a credential or at best with a college degree, but without real academic-intellectual development or skills, and without a moral compass or a values rudder to enable them to navigate successfully in an increasingly complex, chaotic, and often dangerous society beset with problems such as the decline of the family, the increasingly widespread destructiveness of alcohol and other drugs, fatal AIDS and other sexually transmitted diseases, violent crime, and many other problems of similar magnitude. Thus, the worst sin is the cumulative result of the first eighteen deadly sins.

Sin 20: But there is yet another sin competing for the title of "worst": the astounding upward spiral of costs to students, assessed by universities and colleges in spite of their cavalier, woeful performance as educators. As indicated earlier, tuition at public four-year colleges and universities rose 234 percent between 1980–81 and 1994–95, according to a report released in August of 1996 by Congress' General Accounting Office. During the same period, median household income rose 82 percent and the cost of consumer goods rose 74 percent.

EDUCATIONAL FRAUD

Does the stimulation of sky-high expectations by many colleges and universities and their failure to make even a serious effort to deliver on those expectations, while charging outrageous prices—does this constitute fraud?

And does the hiding of the woeful performance of undergraduate education behind the highly publicized facade of outstanding achievement in research, graduate schools, and professional schools exacerbate the suggested fraud?

Whether fraud or some other term is used to characterize the thumbnail description of the "sins" of undergraduate education, the ills presented and others that will be discussed throughout this book should elicit strong emotions from readers.

Without the transformation of the emotional reactions of students, their parents, legislators, taxpayers, and donors into a powerful surge of widespread protest, the weak responses to the studies of the 1980s and

1990s will likely be duplicated by weak responses to the studies of the 1990s and beyond. And students and society will be the losers.

The old story about how you get action out of a cantankerous mule seems appropriate here. You whack him on the head with a two-by-four first to get his attention. Hopefully the surge of protest stimulated by the higher education studies, especially the 1998 Boyer Commission report, and this book will be the two-by-four which will get the attention of the academic community so that it can be nudged into a full-scale regeneration of undergraduate education. Hopefully some of our leaders can be convinced to wield a two-by-four.

The potential is certainly there. U.S. colleges and universities are collectively a tremendous reservoir of superior intellect and expertise, and have been responsible for establishing world leadership in research, the best graduate schools in the world, and the best professional schools.

If that superior intellect and expertise were directed in a totally committed effort toward "fixing" undergraduate education, it seems a foregone conclusion that U.S. undergraduate education would, in the not too distant future, also be the best in the world, and more than adequately meet the critical needs of society.

Stimulation of the academic community by an aroused public to concerted action-reform is imperative, but it will not be enough. Strong participation by the public—in the regeneration process and in ongoing governance—will be needed to prevent what Newman described earlier: "Left totally to its own, the university will evolve toward self-interest, rather than public interest."

THE CALL TO ACTION

Most of the studies referred to in this book describe a serious crisis in undergraduate education and call for strong measures, as did the Boyer Commission report and the Wingspread study.

The report of the study of the American Association of Colleges said, regarding urgency: ". . . the recent critiques and analyses of American education are as vital to clarifying our condition as were the pamphlets of Tom Paine before the American Revolution and the speeches of Abraham Lincoln on the eve of the Civil War."

George Keller said in *Academic Strategy*: "What is needed is a rebirth of academic management. . . ." Ernest Boyer, on behalf of the Carnegie Foundation study (in the mid-eighties), stated, "The American college is, we believe, ready for renewal, and there is urgency to the task." The AAC urges strong and widespread reform, as did the National Institute of Education in its study report. The 1994 Wingspread report described an even greater urgency in the need for change, calling for "renewal" and "radical reformation" of undergraduate education.

The Boyer Commission report in 1998 states: "We believe that the state of undergraduate education at research universities is such a crisis, an issue of such magnitude and volatility that universities must galvanize themselves to respond." And they must respond now.

All the studies and considerable expert opinion will be referred to from time to time throughout the book.

PART TWO

DOGMATIC, RADICAL RECOMMENDATIONS FOR REFORM

PREFACE TO PART TWO

Having determined in the first five chapters that extensive reform of higher education is imperative, a number of major obstacles to reform and a much greater number of recommendations for overcoming the obstacles are presented in part 2.

The labeling of each recommendation as "radical" may be misleading, because most readers are likely to find little they consider radical. On the other hand, some academics will consider some recommendations not only radical, but dangerous heresy; and some governing board members and even more so, board staff, will have great concern about some recommendations they consider radical, but they will be different recommendations than those that concern academics.

Since a primary aim of this book is to stimulate serious dialogue that will lead to significant reform, it is expected that there will be much stronger reaction to the specific, dogmatic presentation of the "radical recommendations" than there would have been to a presentation of only a number of alternatives in response to a particular problem or obstacle.

Except for the first obstacle and recommendation in part 2, which deal with a general, overall topic, all other obstacles and recommendations will be presented under the appropriate of the following category headings: a general concern, governance, leadership, the faculty role, teaching, probing deep into teaching and learning, the academic program, conduct, and finances.

Occasionally and appropriately, a topic and a similar recommendation will appear under two or more of the category headings. For example, eliminating the expectation that all faculty will be productive researchers will change the role of many faculty; it will increase attention to teaching, and it will be a financial boon to the institution. Therefore, the topic will be dealt with under the headings: the faculty role, teaching, and finances.

As a matter of fact, the teaching-research dilemma is such a central issue in reform that it will be dealt with in a number of recommendations.

Radical Recommendation 1
Reverse Homogenization Trend

Work to develop a horizontal system of higher education in which each institution would carve out its own niche and seek prestige and distinction through the excellence it exhibits in carrying out its own mission and goals.

SEVEN

GOVERNANCE

E xternal factors influencing the decline of diversity and of autonomy
are (1) centralization of authority in systems offices away from the
campuses in the system, (2) formula funding systems, and (3) accrediting
agencies.

EXTERNAL GOVERNANCE

Obstacle #2
Centralization of Authority

In the 1977 national meeting of the presidents of the 325 institutions
belonging to the American Association of State Colleges and Universities, a resolution was passed which, in part, said:

"[T]he Association believes that excessive state regulation and intrusion into the internal management of colleges and universities are counter-
productive and expensive for higher education and the American public
as is federal regulation and intrusion."

This concern continued through the 1980s and beyond as many presidents and other observers saw governing board staffs of systems as a principle concern in the diminishing of campus autonomy. The mushrooming
staffs usurped authority from the campuses, thereby crippling the campus
initiative and creativity, and they also got board approval for policies cov-
ering all campuses that forced conformity and similarity.

This diminishment of diversity and campus autonomy will make it
very difficult for campuses to do a Wingspread campus assessment and
develop a campus plan for reform.

Radical Recommendation 2
Centralization

Change the role of systems' board staffs from administering the institutions and providing policy proposals to the board, to serving the needs of the board by providing relevant information and advice to the board.

This would eliminate the highly centralized board staff bureaucracy and return more autonomy to the campuses. However, each campus president must then be held strictly accountable for managing his or her campus in compliance with the board policy and directives.

Radical Recommendation 3

Slash the size of the board staffs to a relative few individuals, since staff responsibilities will have been greatly reduced.

With a greatly reduced board staff, will the board receive the assistance it needs to govern effectively? As a matter of fact, relieved of administrative responsibility over the campuses and the development of policy recommendations, the staff can concentrate on serving the needs of the board and likely improve their service.

With only a skeletal board staff, how can the lay board get the considerable professional expertise it will need? The campuses are stocked with bright people with expertise in many areas.

For example, campus presidents are likely members of the American Association of State Colleges and Universities (and/or other higher education organizations), which keeps them currently informed through national meetings, workshops, service centers, consulting services, and publications, all addressing institutions' concerns, problems, and innovations.

Similarly, vice presidents for business and finance likely are members of the National Association of College and University Business Officers, which also provides many services to its members, including a monthly magazine, and *College and University Business Administration*, a several-volume, loose-leaf, continually updated publication which is virtually the bible for college business and finance officers.

There are a great many other nonfaculty and faculty expert groups on the campuses.

These groups could be convened as needed to provide expert advice, guidance, and recommendations to the board. Technological developments make it possible to have such meetings without anyone having to leave his or her campus, providing great savings in travel costs and time.

Radical Recommendation 4

If there are a large number of institutions under a governing board, create more boards, preferably by type of institution supervised.

Boards are not expensive, because board members serve without pay. The cost of very small board staffs should not be a deterrent to the addition of one or two or even three additional boards, because of the benefit that could result from adding more boards.

Board members with only one type of institution and fewer institutions to govern can get to understand the type, and each individual institution better, and therefore be better able to govern according to society's needs.

Coordination between boards should be maintained by having a representative of the coordinating board and a representative of each governing board be a nonvoting member of each other board.

Additionally, the appointing of more board members will provide more lay persons knowledgeable about higher education—its accomplishments, problems, and needs—who can represent it authoritatively to other state officials and the general public.

The discussion thus far on external governance has centered on state institutions. In his 1987 book, *Choosing Quality*, Dr. Frank Newman quotes organizational expert Dr. Clark Kerr as saying: "The governance of systems is one of the really sore points in American higher education." It is a sore point also for the Wingspread Group's recommendations, and thus is being given considerable attention here.

The book *Choosing Quality* was the result of a governance study funded by the Ford Foundation and the Andrew Mellon Foundation and copyrighted by the Education Commission of the States.

In the book, Newman says about the systems, "There is a tendency to level . . . campuses down so that all campuses look more alike and lose their diversity.

"There is also a tendency for the campus to lose academic autonomy (and consequently flexibility and initiative) to the system."

Newman's concerns about systems are especially relevant to those systems with a large number of institutions under the supervision of one board. Such a system is likely to have a chancellor, and numerous vice chancellors, associate vice chancellors, assistant chancellors, analysts ad infinitum, and a large number of support staff.

Such a staff tends to be a buffer, insulating the board from contact with the campuses and the many bright, knowledgeable experts there.

In *Choosing Quality*, Newman urges more institutional autonomy, but he is quick to point out the other side of the coin, as we indicated earlier. He says: "Left totally to its own, the university will evolve toward self-interest, rather than public interest."

A final component for the provision of effective external governance is the board member.

Radical Recommendation 5

Board members should not be appointed because they gave strong support to the governor's election campaign or to the party.

Rather, they should be selected for their achievements, their leadership potential, their character, and their interest in providing meaningful public service.

On being appointed, they should attend one or more training sessions for board members conducted by the Association of Governing Boards.

Properly selected and prepared board members, having knowledge about the smaller number of institutions they govern, and having direct contact with presidents and others from the campuses, should be able to guide campus personnel to keep their focus on serving the needs of society, while encouraging them through the provision of greater flexibility to utilize the campuses' creativity in the process.

More such initial and continuing lay involvement is essential for the rejuvenation of undergraduate education so that society's needs may be well met.

Obstacle #3
Formula Funding Systems

Many states have used formulas for determining the levels of funding for the state's institutions. The usual formula is student driven. For example, the basis would be the number of full-time equivalent students enrolled the preceding year, with the amount per student varying depending on the level of the courses and the discipline in which they were taken. Freshman-level courses would be funded at a lesser level than senior courses, and engineering courses would be funded at a higher level than education courses. Other categories such as libraries are also included.

Such a formula strongly influences standardization of programs and operations across campuses. And since the preceding year's categories and enrollment levels determine the next year's funding levels, the formula can be a real deterrent to innovation.

For example, a number of years ago a state university built a fantastic learning resources center that provided unique learning technology, support staff, and instructional development experts to assist the faculty to new heights in teaching effectiveness.

There was no comparable facility in the state (or in nearby states) so there was no funding category in the formula for a learning resources center. On appealing to the coordinating board, the university was told it would have to use money from that appropriated to operate the library to operate the LRC, leaving the library greatly underfunded.

The university was penalized for being innovative when it should have been rewarded for its creative effort to vastly improve undergraduate instruction.

Radical Recommendation 6
Formula Funding

Provide more flexibility in formula funding systems so that innovation can be encouraged and even rewarded, or discard the formula system for a better way to allocate state funds to state institutions.

Obstacle #4
Accrediting Agencies

There are six regional accrediting agencies (Southern Association of Colleges and Schools, North Central Association of Colleges and Schools, etc.) which accredit entire institutions, and about forty discipline accrediting bodies (National Association of Schools of Music, American Assembly of Collegiate Schools of Business, National League for Nursing, etc.) that evaluate and accredit programs within institutions.

Regional accrediting agencies to some degree get involved in internal matters that can influence an institution which is being evaluated to conform to generally standardized structures or procedures. For example, a librarian who was a member of a visiting committee told the university being visited that the campus learning resources center director should report to the university librarian instead of to the academic vice president, since the LRC was a lesser academic support unit than the library. Never mind that the librarian had virtually no knowledge about the LRC.

Some of the discipline accrediting associations can be very restrictive to institutions seeking accreditation or reaccreditation of one of their programs.

Often there is rigidity in regard to specific courses, course sequences, course levels, research productivity of faculty, number of faculty with Ph.D. degrees, faculty salaries, facilities, etc.

Institutions sometimes are reluctant to try new instructional techniques, innovative course patterns, interdisciplinary courses, and other deviations from the norm for fear of jeopardizing their accreditation.

For example: In an area where music recording, publishing, and performing were very prominent, a local university's president and others from the university met with prominent members of the music community to see if there was some specific way the university could serve the music industry.

The music people said that they didn't need the university to train more "pickers and singers." They said they needed middle management people—people with fiscal, management, advertising, and public relations skills—with an understanding of the music business, including the recording business.

The university shortly established a committee with a member from each of the three areas—the music department, the journalism department, and the school of business. The aim was to forge an interdisciplinary program with courses from each of the three areas. In which area would the program be housed? It soon became evident that such an interdisciplinary program could not be listed as a music or a business program because it would jeopardize the accreditation of the music department or the school of business.

Radical Recommendation 7
Accrediting Agencies

Organizations of colleges and universities should strongly urge accrediting agencies to examine the goals of an institution or a particular program, and compare the results to the goals. Accrediting bodies should not get involved in the structure and operation of an institution, or the structure and content of individual programs.

INTERNAL GOVERNANCE

Internal governance of American colleges and universities has been described in such widely divergent terms as presidential dictatorships to organized anarchies.

If higher education is to make effective response to Wingspread and the Boyer Commission's call for great change in higher education in order for it to meet the awesome challenges of the early twenty-first century, there will need to be an internal as well as an external restructuring.

Obstacle #5
Governance Myths

Professor and researcher Hazard Adams says that a myth persists of a "Golden Age" in U.S. history "when a condition of faculty control and Athenian self-government did exist on most campuses."

"Except in a few rare instances, no such time ever existed," says

George Keller in *Academic Strategy*, a report of a study on management funded by the Carnegie Corporation and published in cooperation with the American Association of Higher Education.

Keller continues: "Throughout most of the history of American higher education, clergymen, politicians, merchants, pedagogical entrepreneurs, and autocratic presidents have run the colleges, often with a stern grip."

Size of institutions mitigates against faculty governance. Earlier studies showed that the majority of faculty members are in institutions enrolling more than ten thousand students, and some institutions enroll more than fifty thousand.

Keller reports in his study that faculty tend to be focused predominantly on their own specialized activities rather than departmental problems, school or college problems, or matters of university-wide significance. And another factor is that the professorate is split into separate faculties of arts and science, engineering, law, business, medicine, and agriculture that further narrows their focus and separates them from colleagues in other major academic units.

In spite of these factors, a move to shared governance began to gain momentum in the 1950s and continued in successive decades. The movement was based on the belief of many faculties in the mistaken idea of the already discussed historical precedent in U.S. education, and equally erroneous beliefs about "faculty governance in English and German higher education."

In addition, the American Association of University Professors, initially primarily concerned with "faculty rights" such as academic freedom and tenure, began to urge faculties to seek control over "their area" to keep administration out of academic affairs.

Radical Recommendation 8
Faculty in Governance

The exposure of the myth of faculty's historic right to govern; the vastly increased size of colleges and universities; the separation of faculties into departmental, school, and college units; the absorption of faculty in their own individual activities; and the reluctance of faculty to make "hard decisions" indicate a diminished decision-making

role for faculty. **A better system of internal governance must be designed.**

Obstacle #6
Emulation of Prestige Institutions

The prestige institutions are generally thought to be in the vanguard of the faculty governance movement. There seems to be a desire at many institutions to imitate the perceived internal operations and structure as well as the research productivity of research universities.

Radical Recommendation 9
One System for All

Homogenization of internal governance structure should be discouraged because institutions vary so much in size, mission, role, and scope that no one governance structure is practical for all.

Obstacle #7
Adversarial Relationships
On some campuses practicing faculty governance over academic matters, there appears to be a paralyzing adversarial relationship between faculty and administration.

Radical Recommendation 10
Internal Gridlock

The president, with the backing of the governing board, must initiate dialogue with administration and faculty toward the development of a greater role for management. This is in line with what Keller found in his study, *Academic Strategy*: "The faculty-administration stalemate of the postwar period is yielding with reluctant speed to a clearer authority for the executive and more active leadership from management."

While more administrative leadership and decision making is called for here, this does not imply less involvement in leadership and decision making by faculty, but rather a different kind of involvement. This will become evident in the following discussion about how planning and change in colleges and universities has come about in the past, and how these things need to be approached now if there is to be hope that the massive change called for by Wingspread and the Boyer Commission can be achieved.

Obstacle #8
Process for Change

Probably few, if any, campuses have in place a process and a structure to expeditiously plan for massive changes.

Radical Recommendation 11
Change

Planning and decision making for change must be vastly improved.

Obstacle #9
Incrementalism Dominance

In the post–World War II decade, management science—systematic, data-based management—made great strides in American society but was not widely embraced by colleges and universities because, critics said, it overlooked the human factor.

Incrementalism—"the science of muddling through"—was the form of planning long used by nearly all campus administrators. Keller explains: "Change comes about, say incrementalists, through hundreds of tiny little steps, no one of which is heavy-footed enough to rock the boat. . . . The steps need to consider self-interest and people's territories." They often require bargaining. Incrementalism is usually consensual.

In *Academic Strategy*, Keller says that a search for a third way in planning has led directly to the creation of the new field of strategic planning.

"Strategic planning," he explains, "attempts to use the best wisdom of both the rational-economic and the partisan political."

Much too simply put, in strategic planning an institution continually examines the external environment—the changing society—and identifies the developing threats and opportunities; it thoroughly examines itself—its history, traditions, strengths, and weaknesses—and it modifies itself—its programs and structure—in a continuous effort to maintain its character while improving its quality and uniqueness, to establish and maintain a competitive position in the highly competitive field of higher education.

Strategic planning does not seek to develop an extensive, detailed, one-time master plan, although it could serve as a vehicle to initiate the extensive, major reform called for by the Wingspread Group and the Boyer Commission. Strategic planning is a process—a continuous, ongoing process.

Less institutional decision making by faculty was recommended earlier, but in strategic planning, faculty should be asked to play a much greater role in helping to guide the university on its future course.

Everyone in the campus community, in addition to alumni and local legislators should be invited to participate and should be thoroughly schooled on the strategic planning process and its goals. Instead of only the president and a few advisers, many good and creative minds should continually be alertly seeking to provide valuable input into the process.

Radical Recommendation 12
Planning

Forcefully institute the strategic planning process.

Obstacle #10
Exclusion of Other Personnel

It is customary on college and university campuses to find a near-total lack of involvement of nonacademic and nonprofessional personnel in seeking institutional improvement.

Many of these people understand their jobs and their areas better than top-level administrators and can often provide ideas about how to improve performance in their areas, and thereby improve institutional performance.

The Quality Circle concept was developed in this country, but used more widely and effectively in business and industry in Japan.

Usually a quality circle is composed of seven to ten people within an institution who do similar work. They meet voluntarily on a regular basis to identify and analyze sources of problems, to recommend solutions to the administration, and, where possible, to implement solutions.

Through the quality circle process, staff may make useful input into the planning process, and most assuredly can help the institution operate more efficiently.

Radical Recommendation 13
Quality Circles

Initiate the quality circle process within the institution.

The Wingspread Group urges institutional assessment and development of a plan for a major overhaul of the institution, both, of course, with the expectation that the plan will be effectively implemented.

Undoubtedly many faculty teach their courses without any thought to the institution's goals as stated in the catalog. So, also, many staff members routinely perform their duties each day with little or no thought to how what they do affects the total institution's performance of its objectives.

If a brilliant plan for the rejuvenation of an institution is developed, it will come to nothing, or at least its implementation will be severely crippled, by the type of lackadaisical, ill-informed performance of faculty and staff described above.

Management by objectives (MBO) may be the answer. MBO is described by management expert Stephen P. Robbins as "a philosophy of management . . . that seeks to convert organizational goals to personal goals to satisfactory performance outcomes."

The organization's objectives at a college or university would likely be established with widespread participation. Once established, the objectives would be pushed down through all levels of the organization.

Robbins says further that objectives will be general for the organization as a whole, but as they cascade down through the levels of the organization they become more focused and specific as they reach individuals. MBO is a philosophy which encourages increased participation in the management of the affairs of the organization at all levels.

Radical Recommendation 14
Management by Objectives

Institute a management by objectives philosophy and process to insure that each person understands his or her role in relation to the institution's objectives, and is evaluated on his or her performance of his or her specific role.

Obstacle #11
Resistance to Business Practices

If a college or university is to be truly regenerated, it must overhaul not only its academic operation, but also its nonacademic functions. Too often higher education institutions arrogantly eschew the practices of business.

It's true that colleges and universities are different from businesses. The primary aim of colleges and universities is service, through educating of students, producing research, and providing public service.

The primary aim of business is to make a profit.

A business for profit would hone its operation to the bare bones. Anything that didn't contribute to making a profit would be trimmed off. Not so in higher education. Department, division, college, and other unit heads are often permitted to "empire build"—to expand without regard to whether the expansion is a justifiable, cost-efficient improvement of the product.

Radical Recommendation 15
Business Practices

Continually examine practices of businesses for profit, looking for ways to maximize the institution's effectiveness in achieving its goals by getting more for its money.

Colleges and universities must reform their "organized anarchies" if there is to be real hope that they can meet the challenges described by the Wingspread Group and the Boyer Commission.

A PLAN

The overall governance and coordination of all post-secondary state education institutions within a state have been a vexing problem for many years. The following example would seem to be an ideal external governance and coordination structure plan for states with a number of state colleges and universities.

Reorganize the state colleges and universities into systems by function and category, with each system having its own governing board, and all institutions being subject to coordination by a coordinating commission.

For example: A state with one research university and one comprehensive university should place them under one board. If it had six regional universities, they should be governed by another board. If it had eight community colleges, they should be governed by another board. If it had six technical institutes, they should be governed by still another board. A state with a similar number and dispersion of institutions governs all in a hodgepodge mix under two boards.

The governing boards should have the authority and responsibility for the operation of the institutions. The coordinating commission would have no operational authority, but would be responsible for: (1) developing a master plan for all state-sponsored higher education; (2) developing a funding system; (3) making a proposal for the funding of all state higher education to the governor and the legislature each year; (4) approving all new programs, new departments, new schools, and new colleges before implementation in individual institutions; (5) preparing a priority list of building needs for the governor and the legislature; and (6) in conjunction with the appropriate governing board, phasing out existing programs that have become obsolete and/or nonproductive.

Finally, the executive director of each board and the coordinating commission would be ex officio members of each other board, thereby facilitating communication between the boards and the commission.

Advantages of the Plan

This plan would present operational, representational, and cost advantages over the current structure of external governance.

Board members would be dealing with similar institutions, so they could develop an understanding of the type; and they would be dealing with a relatively small number of institutions, so they could know each institution better. And there would be more lay input into higher education, increasing the likelihood that the needs of society would be emphasized, rather than the ambitions and desires of educators. The overall result would be more perceptive and effective external governance.

In addition, the greater number of board members would provide a larger number of more knowledgeable lay representatives and advocates for higher education to the general populace, and to other branches of government.

Adding governing boards would seem to increase considerably the cost of governance, but actually the opposite is intended.

Radical recommendation 2 proposes: "Change the role of the systems' board staffs from administering the institutions and providing policy proposals to the board, to serving the needs of the board by providing relevant information and advice to the board."

Radical recommendation 3 suggests: "Slash the size of board staffs to a relative few, since staff responsibilities will have been greatly reduced."

Board members are nonsalaried. Only their expenses to board meetings are paid. It is the large staffs of governing boards—chancellors, vice chancellors, assistant vice chancellors, program analysts, etc.—that are costly, and it is the intent of this recommendation to eliminate most of these paid staff positions. To put it in perspective, the annual salary for one staff position could likely pay the meeting expenses of board members for an entire year.

The Board Staff Dilemma

Early in the development of a system of universities and/or colleges, a chief administrator is generally appointed. If this person's title is chancellor, then campus heads are called presidents; if the system head is called president, then campus heads are chancellors.

Whether the title be chancellor or president, it seems it is the rare system head who, early in his or her tenure, does not seek to expand his or her power at the expense of the campus heads. As more and more power is assumed by the system head, more and more assistants are "needed" to share the growing responsibilities. Soon there are board staff members with assistants and support staff for virtually every category of administration on the campuses.

Much board staff activity duplicates what is already being done on the campuses, often by persons better qualified than board staff.

Also, board staff seem to have a penchant for calling numerous meetings involving campus staff, and for requesting voluminous reports and studies from campus personnel, all of which requires considerable faculty and staff time on the campuses. In fact, campuses have often hired additional personnel in order to meet the demands of board staff.

Not only is the proliferation of board staff inefficient and costly, it also intrudes on campus autonomy and is destructive of internal campus governance systems.

Customarily, the legally constituted governing board of a state institution delegates the authority for the operation of a campus to the campus head—president or chancellor—who in turn delegates authority for specific activity to individuals and groups on the campus.

When board staff with responsibility in a particular area of institutional activity deal directly with personnel on a campus with responsibility in the same activity area, institutional autonomy and the internal governance structure of the campus are subverted.

For example, when faculty members in an academic department on a campus are developing a new program to add to the department's offerings, notification is provided to the chief board staff officer—chancellor or president. A board staff member—perhaps an assistant academic vice chancellor or even a program analyst—will likely be dispatched to the campus to discuss the program with the involved faculty. In some such scenario, the board staffer will exert influence over the program, superseding the campus departmental, college, curricular committee, dean, academic vice president, and president review process.

There is no intent here to imply that governing board staff do not render some valuable service to the board. But too often they also duplicate work being done on the campuses, needlessly increase campus staff and faculty workloads, and discourage initiative and creativity on the campuses by increasing centralization of authority to board staff.

The question might be asked, if there is to be a great reduction in board staff as recommended earlier, will there, then, be a void in the "valuable services" provided to the board?

No, not at all. In fact, if the role of the board staff is to provide services to the board, not to be a "super-administrative staff" with authority over all the campuses, then services to the board will likely be improved.

And board performance can be expected to improve also under the increased-board plan. Boards with only one type of institution to supervise can be expected to become knowledgeable about that type of institution. For example, a board responsible for six regional universities should gain a good understanding of what a regional university is and how it functions. Contrast that with a situation where the board supervises the operation of forty-six institutions consisting of six distinct types—comprehensive research university, regional university, community college, technical community college, technical institute, and vocational school.

Returning to the issue of board staff, the question might be asked, will a very small board staff have the experience and knowledge to provide the board with all the expertise it will need in order to govern effectively? Probably not, but there is considerable expertise on the campuses which the boards can utilize.

For example, look at the regional universities currently governed by the Tennessee Board of Regents.

Most, if not all, of the presidents have been members of the American Association of State Colleges and Universities. AASCU provides its members several-day annual meetings, summer week-long workshops, consulting services, and publications, all addressing institutions' concerns, problems, and innovations. In addition, each campus head almost certainly holds an earned doctor's degree, and has had experience in some, if not all, of the following positions: teacher and researcher, department chairperson, dean, and vice president.

A council of these presidents, meeting periodically and at the call of the board, could provide information, understanding, advice, and recommendations likely superior to board staff input.

The chief board staff officer—executive director or executive secretary—could, at the direction of the board, convene and chair the Presidents' Council. This person, who would not be an administrative officer over the institutions, should, however, be a trusted and highly valued source of information and counsel for the board. On occasion, the board might choose to delegate temporary administrative authority over an institution to the executive director to deal with a specific situation.

In addition to the Presidents' Council, the executive director might convene and chair a council of vice presidents for business and finance from the universities. Likely, these vice presidents are members of the National Association of College and University Business Officers, which boasts about two thousand nonprofit higher education institution members. NACUBO's activities center around the following areas: (1) providing professional development programs for business officers through workshops and seminars; (2) producing a wide range of publications to meet the profession's information needs; (3) improving methods of financial and business management; (4) monitoring and interpreting government activity that affects colleges and universities; and (5) providing information services to its members and others.

Among its publications are the monthly *Business Officer* magazine; a book, *NACUBO Writers on Financial Management*, which is a compilation of the best *Business Officer* articles; and *College and University Business Administration*, a several-volume, loose-leaf publication which is virtually the bible for college business and finance officers. As changes occur in various areas of activity, NACUBO mails updated chapters to be inserted in the loose-leaf volumes.

A council of chief institutional fiscal officers could be a tremendous source of information, advice, and recommendations to the board on fiscal matters.

Then there is the great number of outstanding specialist-experts on the faculties of the institutions. Boards have rarely learned to tap this vast resource of diverse expertise for the benefit of the system of institutions and for society.

Finally, there are a great many other nonfaculty experts—computer center directors, campus planners, etc.—on the campus who could be convened by the board's executive director to provide advice and guidance to the board.

Summary of "The Plan"

With responsibility for a smaller number of institutions, and only like institutions, board members could know their institutions much better. And with a much smaller board staff, but a staff totally devoted to assisting the board rather than trying to administer a large number of institutions, the board should be able to provide considerably more enlightened, effective governance.

The money saved because of the much smaller board staffs could go to the campuses to improve the education of students. And the dismantling of the huge systems' stifling central bureaucracy would encourage creativity and innovation on the campuses and do wonders for campus morale—the basis for a high level of productive effectiveness.

Higher education could well use the increased number of board members who would be a more knowledgeable group of advocates for higher education to other state officials and to the public.

Difficulty of External Change

Realistically, "the plan" could be expected to bring about the improvements as described. Realistically also, the likelihood of such a plan being implemented is remote, because of political factors.

Regardless of whether all, some, or none of "the plan" is implemented, educators, politicians, and concerned citizens should continually strive to achieve the goals of the plan. Whatever the external structure, doing major surgery on central board administrative bureaucracy; cutting board staff costs; enabling board members to become more knowledgeable about higher education and the institutions they govern; utilizing campus expertise more in the governing process; decreasing or eliminating board staff involvement in internal institutional matters; and providing more autonomy to the campuses, thereby stimulating creativity, innovation, and high morale on the campuses—these should be the continuing goals.

COORDINATION

Most of "the plan" and the discussion of it center on governance, but coordination is equally important. Each individual institution cannot be permitted to become all that it might wish to be—or all that its geographic community might wish it to be.

For instance: each regional university in a state may want to have a medical school, a veterinary medicine school, or other of the tremendously high-cost programs. And they each may want a full range of doctoral programs, also very costly.

And each community college may wish to become a four-year college or a university.

Some communities that do not have a higher education institution may wish to have a college or a university.

States do not have the financial resources to satisfy the higher education wishes of every institution or community. So, initial as well as periodic decisions must be made about how best to meet the higher education needs of the state within the maximum financial resources the state can provide.

As has been pointed out, states cannot afford to provide each community with a university offering a full range of undergraduate, graduate, and professional programs, though most states can offer most of the range of programs needed, but not the number of each program desired.

So the basic concern of coordination has to be the number of duplicate programs the state can afford and where they should be placed to most fairly serve the needs of the state's citizens.

A number of years ago, a large but somewhat sparsely populated state with very limited resources maintained one state university and six state colleges. It assigned some mainstream undergraduate degree programs exclusively to specific colleges. For example, only one institution (college A) offered undergraduate degrees in music, while another distant college (college B) was the only one offering degrees in physical education. Studies, of course, showed that nearly 90 percent of those in the state earning degrees in music lived within reasonable proximity to college A (which offered degrees in music), and a similar large percentage of those earning degrees in physical education lived in the area in which college B was located. Ideally, a state would wish to make programs in both music and physical education equally available to all qualified residents of the state regardless of where they lived.

Most four-year state institutions now offer degrees in both music and physical education, but in each state, certain specialized, expensive under-graduate and graduate programs are limited to one or a few of the state's higher education institutions. The range of programs and their availability and convenience to students within the state's ability to pay are the con-tinuing concerns of a coordinating agency.

EIGHT

LEADERSHIP

THE PRESIDENT AND THE BOARD

No significant, widespread institutional reform can take place without the enthusiastic backing of the governing board and the institution's president.

The board will provide authority for the reform process, and will certainly require periodic reports on the status of the process. It might even be well to have one or more board members involved in the process to guide it in the direction of society's needs as opposed to institutional ambitions.

Recommended structures of governing boards, and qualifications of board members were discussed under the heading of external governance.

Much of the discussion here will be focused on the president—his or her qualifications, role, and conditions of the position.

"The position of the college or university president as a force in education continues to decline."

This statement could be from one of the relatively recent studies of the American college or university presidency, but it's not. Rather, it was written by Dr. Harold Dodd, former president of Princeton University and published in his 1962 work titled *The Academic President: Educator or Caretaker.*

Obstacle #12
Inadequate Presidential Leadership

A study by the Association of Governing Boards (AGB) says that American colleges and universities are suffering from a pervasive lack of strong presidential leadership. AGB study chairman Dr. Clark Kerr says that institutions need leadership most when faced with a period of rapid change.

Surely presidential leadership is of tremendous importance as institutions prepare to embark on the assessment and major renovation called for in this book. Therefore, considerable attention will be given here to the presidency and the president.

Radical Recommendation 16
Strengthen the Presidency

College and university presidencies must be strengthened in order that the presidents can provide strong leadership to their institutions as they prepare to consider vast change.

But, where to begin? The AGB study points the way, as chairman Kerr explains that the leadership void the study group found "was more of a function of unfavorable circumstances surrounding the presidency than of the caliber of the people currently serving in the office."

The AGB study contends that "the basic problem is that the president's job at many institutions has become too difficult, too stressful, too constrained by outside influences, and too unrewarding to attract or long retain the kind of person who is probably best qualified to serve."

In the mid-1980s, the John Minter Associates did a study of the presidency for the *Chronicle of Higher Education.* The study concluded that presidents are spending more and more time away from their campuses raising money and defending their institutions to a skeptical public. Some specific responses from presidents in the study follow:

- "The pressures from external agencies have increased tremendously in the last few years."
- "More demanding publics to serve; tighter, far more cumbersome external controls."
- "Much more external political pressure and intrusion."
- "Much more time spent in being accountable. Less time for imaginative leadership. Paperwork can overwhelm one."

Obstacle #13
Conditions of the Presidency

What can be done to change the conditions of the presidency to enable presidents to function as leaders, especially in a time of anticipated great change? Some suggestions follow.

Radical Recommendations 17–24
Alter Conditions of the Presidency

17. The governing board should endeavor to protect the president and the institution from outside interference.
18. The board also should not meddle in the internal campus affairs.
19. The board should make sure that the president has an adequate and competent staff that can provide him or her with assistance in dealing with external matters and provide relief from the more mundane internal tasks, so that the president can concentrate on the major responsibilities—especially leadership—which should be handled by the president.
20. A lay board should have a president in whom they have confidence, and they should support him or her.
21. The board should make it clear to all of the institution's employees that they report to and are responsible to the president. The board should discourage the faculty or staff from circumventing the president and coming to individual board members about institutional matters.
22. Job security should be provided by several-year (preferably five) contracts, which would likely encourage presidents to initiate plans and programs that might not come to fruition for at least several years, rather than concentrating exclusively on the immediate in order to protect job security from month to month.
23. The president should be evaluated on his or her long-term record, not just in terms of one group or one problem or at one point in time.
24. Remuneration and other benefits for the president should be increased to a level that will facilitate the hiring and retention of persons with the ability, vision, knowledge, and strength to fill one

of the most difficult, stressful, significant positions in our society—
that of college or university presidency.

Obstacle #14
Flawed Presidents

There are presidents who are inadequate for the major leadership role required in institutional rejuvenation.

A presidency is not a part-time job. It can use all the time the president can physically devote to it, and still need more. It would be a rare president who could spend much time keeping current in his narrow area of specialization, continuing to do research and writing in his or her field without cheating the presidency of time it needs.

Some presidents immerse themselves in the daily detail of finances and operational matters, creating a leadership void.

Some presidents have been very dominant, even dictatorial on campus, squelching faculty initiative and denying themselves the benefit of input from their many bright, specialist colleagues.

One very intelligent, talented scholar-teacher who, as president, faced problems by gathering information, consulting, discussing and deliberating endlessly, was seemingly unable to conclude the process by making needed decisions.

Then there is the exuberant cheerleader type who "talks a good game"—says the things people want to hear—but provides little substance or action.

Institutions planning to accept the Wingspread and the Boyer Commission challenges for change will need to have or seek presidents with most if not all of the following recommended characteristics and abilities.

Radical Recommendations 25–33
Presidential Characteristics and Abilities

25. **The president must be a generalist—the only true generalist in the college or university. All others represent some unit within the institution. As such, the president must have some understanding of all the disciplines and units within the institution.**

As a generalist, the president must perform a role similar to that of a symphony conductor. The conductor works to get each musician, regardless of her instrument, to give her best individual performance in a coordinated effort to produce a beautiful orchestral rendition.

Similarly, the president must meld the various university individuals and units of diverse expertise into a smoothly functioning, cohesive organization working toward the common goal of effectively fulfilling the university's mission.

26. A president should be a well-informed generalist with knowledge about his institution, higher education, and societal problems and trends if he is to provide leadership in reviewing the institution's mission and reevaluating its goals in an ongoing strategic planning process.

He continually needs to lead the search for answers to: What should our college or university be doing? How should it be doing it? How can it do it better?

27. The president should be a visionary and stimulate others to be forward looking also.

28. The president should be a leader. Effective presidents seldom lead by the power of their office. They lead by their ability to marshall the facts and present their arguments persuasively.

29. A president must be an excellent communicator. An intelligent president with great knowledge, vision, and wisdom will likely fail if she lacks the ability to communicate.

30. The president must be able to make decisions. He can and should sometimes delegate decision making, but he must not abrogate his decision-making responsibilities.

31. The president should have financial expertise and management skills.

32. The president should be a tone setter. The president can set the tone for the campus by her words and by her performance, stressing: excellence; integrity; fairness; courage; and concern for the institution, the individual, and society.

33. The president must have patience. The seemingly endless consultations and efforts at persuasion, and the sometimes maddening snail's pace of progress would test the patience of Job.

SHARED LEADERSHIP

Few colleges or universities have achieved true distinction without out-standing leader presidents. But institutions are not likely to be even good institutions without effective department chairpersons.

Dr. Allan Tucker says in *Chairing the Academic Department* that "it is the chairperson who must supervise the translation of institutional goals and policies into academic practice."

It is true that the college and university functions—teaching, research, and public service—are performed by faculty under the direct supervision of the chairperson. Quoting William Ouchi in John B. Bennett's 1983 work *Managing the Academic Department*, Thomas A. Emmet says: "The management expert on Z organization and Japanese business theory, William Ouchi, suggests that the smallest working unit is the key to quality and productivity in the industrial setting. It is high time we recognized this fact in higher education."

Tucker says that the chairperson needs to be knowledgeable in three areas: planning, management, and leadership techniques.

Colleges and universities hire Ph.D. graduates to teach although almost none have had any preparation in pedagogy and are seldom given any by the hiring institution.

Similarly, chairpersons are selected from the ranks of the faculty, having had no formal preparation for the chair's role, and rarely are they given any by the appointing institution.

So the real work of the university—teaching and related functions—is done by persons unprepared to teach, and supervised by management unprepared to manage. If higher education is to be significantly improved, attention must be given to these two matters.

Improving teaching will be cursorily and thoroughly discussed in chapters 9 and 10.

Radical Recommendation 34
Administrative Preparation

A course in college administration should be made available to doctoral students with aspirations to some day becoming a department chair-

person, dean, academic vice president, and even president. Each college and university should provide in-service administrative training, especially for department chairpersons—newly appointed or veteran.

The effectiveness of the department is the responsibility of the chairperson, and the effectiveness of the university is the sum of the effectiveness of its departments. So the chair's role is tremendously important.

It is also tremendously difficult. Chairpersons have multiple, often-conflicting roles.

- They must represent central administration and its authority, seeing to it that faculty carry out their functions, and evaluating their performance as well.
- Then they must represent the faculty—their plans, needs, and welfare—to central administration.
- In addition, they must be teaching colleagues, working side by side with faculty.
- Relations with students can be extremely complex for the chairperson of an academic department.
- And the chair is also expected to provide leadership to the department.

Effective evaluation of teaching is crucial to individual and departmental morale, and it is very difficult. Performance evidence such as student ratings and course plans (blueprints) should be carefully examined by the chair and discussed thoroughly with the faculty member.

Consistency in evaluation is important. The chair should not make misleading preevaluating statements. For example, the chair should not, at various times during the academic year, tell the faculty member she is doing a great job, and then rate the professor average or less at evaluation time.

The chairperson should encourage, and praise good performance when praise is warranted. When a chair gives negative evaluation, he should endeavor to use it to help the faculty member improve performance, and this intent should be made clear to the professor.

Throughout her entire performance, but especially in the area of evaluation, it is essential that the chairperson endeavors to establish a reputation for fairness and integrity.

The role of the head of nonacademic units can also be difficult, though generally not nearly as complex as that of the academic chair.

Persons such as the director of admissions and the registrar can provide leadership in their areas, which they probably know better than anyone in the institution.

The admissions head can be alert to concerns the admissions staff hears from the prospective students and their parents, and relay them to other administrators for possible correction of things causing concern.

The registrar can seek to improve the registration process and make it easy for students to use.

Radical Recommendation 35
Team Participation

Maximum improvement in the university can be best facilitated if every employee feels like an important member of "the team" and if this concept is enhanced by the use of MBO, Quality Circles, and strategic planning, as indicated earlier.

Thus, leadership should come from many sources within the college or university.

SHARED LEADERSHIP (OTHER EMPLOYEES)

The importance of faculty, presidents, department chairs, and other unit heads has been discussed, but there are a great many other employees who can have a significant effect on the level of success of a university and who can also provide leadership.

Personnel psychologists tell us that an employee's ego is under assault from the time he enters the workplace until he leaves. The time clock, the ID card, the supervisor, and like regimentation bruise one's ego.

An employee generally spends less than one fourth of his or her total time on the job, but the dehumanizing effect of the job can cripple a person's self-image and have an adverse, demoralizing effect on a person's total life.

Too often management is insensitive to the dehumanizing effect of the workplace. It is important to remember that morale is one of the most important factors in individual performance. And the total of individual performances is what determines institutional success . . . or failure.

Two key words are *concern* and *communication*. Administrators should show concern about the individual as an employee and as a person through two-way communication.

If supervisors frequently discussed with the workers the institutions problems, needs, aspirations, and most emphatically its successes; if they engendered a feeling of pride in their college among the employees, then the employee's performance is likely to be enthusiastic and the employee's contact with their families, friends, neighbors, and others would likely be very beneficial to the institution.

Satisfied students and enthusiastic employees are the best public relations agents a college or a university can have.

It must be pointed out to the employee that:

- Your job can be very boring if you concentrate only on carrying out the routine daily functions. It can be much more interesting if you see your job in the larger context.
- You will get more satisfaction if you are alert to how your contributions help the institution carry out its mission.
- You will get greater satisfaction out of seeing yourself as a team member helping the institution achieve its larger goals.
- And, as you look beyond your job, you will likely be able to come up with improvements in your job that will better serve your department or unit and the larger goals of the college or university.

NINE

THE FACULTY ROLE

In America's first higher education institutions, faculty were clergymen or people who had prepared for the ministry but taught for a few years before going into their church vocations. The role of the faculty was to develop each individual student intellectually, morally, and spiritually—the whole student. The curriculum was the same for each student, and the faculty member, who was a generalist, taught all subjects for his group of students for four years (unless the faculty member did not remain for four years).

Years later career faculty began to appear, as did some minimal specialization, the latter accelerated by the vocational diversity which followed the development of the first land-grant institutions in the 1860s.

Yet even toward the end of the nineteenth century, higher education historian W. H. Cowley tells us that one professor at Northwestern University taught botany, chemistry, geology, Greek, logic, mineralogy, physics, and zoology. But there was a gradual emergence of specialization, so that by 1960 we had not only chemists, but colloid chemists, inorganic colloid chemists, and even high temperature aerosol inorganic chemists, etc.

However, the thing which really changed American education and the role of the faculty was the influx of German-educated Ph.D.s with their intense interest in scholarship and research.

Dominance of research over teaching began to appear. As was pointed out earlier, Abraham Flexner put it graphically in a 1905 speech to a higher education association when he said, "the university had sacrificed college teaching at the altar of research."

Cowley said that, as early as the late 1930s, large numbers of faculty members gave their primary allegiance to research and considered teaching a chore to bypass whenever it interfered with their investigations.

Obstacle #15
Continued Homogenization with Expanded Emphasis of Research over Teaching

In recent years at research universities, as the name indicates, research has become the primary concern of the faculty. In *College*, Ernest Boyer reported that 26 percent of the faculty at those universities did no teaching of undergraduates at all. Others had very light teaching loads, and graduate assistants did much of the teaching.

In 1991 the *Chronicle of Higher Education* reported that interviews with students at more than a dozen of the country's largest research universities revealed that dissatisfaction with undergraduate education was intense and widespread.

Faculty members interviewed for the story said that research and nurturing graduate students took up most of their time. This was recognized by student comment which indicated that with professors, their research comes first and then their attention goes to graduate students. The undergraduate students come last.

Students resent being put in classes of six hundred to one thousand, where students could be no more than passive listeners. And contact with professors by students is rare, as is advising of students about their academic programs, students reported.

In *College*, Boyer says that there is a strong movement among America's diverse institutions to emulate the research universities, and for the faculties to emphasize research over undergraduate teaching—increasing homogenization.

On the faculty's behalf, it must be pointed out that Ph.D. programs rarely prepare prospective faculty to teach, advise students, or participate in institution-wide curriculum development. In addition, graduate professors create graduate students in their own image—specialists in a narrow field of knowledge with well-honed research skills.

It is natural for graduate professors to tell their graduate students to concentrate on research and publishing articles and books when they join a faculty, because the graduate professors receive distinction not only because of their own research and publishing, but also from similar activity by their former students.

Institutional reward systems—tenure, promotion, and significant salary increases—in a great many institutions emphasize research and publication over teaching. Is it any wonder that faculty do likewise?

In a story in the April 15, 1992, *Chronicle of Higher Education*, James S. Fairweather provided evidence about how financial rewards are skewed because of research emphasis. He secured data from 4,332 full-time, tenure-track faculty members at a wide range of four-year institutions. His data shows that:

- "The more time you spend on teaching the less the compensation."
- "The more hours in class per week, the lower the pay."
- "The greater the time spent on research, the higher the compensation."
- "Faculty who teach only graduate students get paid the most."
- "The greater the number of refereed publications, the greater the income."

Fairweather said the analysis of his data documented the domination of research and scholarship in determining how much faculty members are paid, not just in research universities, but in each four-year institutional category.

Fairweather explained, "in most cases teaching productivity is neutral as a factor in compensation, and is simply not rewarded."

"On the whole," Fairweather said, "my analysis supported the widespread belief that institutional drift was accruing in higher education as professors at various types of colleges and universities increasingly sought to emulate the research focus characteristics at leading research institutions." Once again, evidence of homogeneity.

The research-dominated prestige and reward systems have motivated many faculty to steal time from teaching and invest it, often unenthusiastically, into research which not only dilutes the quality of teaching, but also often creates inferior research of little value.

Some will claim that it is necessary for a faculty member to be an active, producing researcher in order to be an effective teacher. This is a myth. A number of research studies have indicated that there is no statistical significant relationship between research productivity and teaching effectiveness.

An extremely succinct and clear analysis of the research-teaching relationship was presented by Rutgers University's Boyan Barnett in the *Chronicle of Higher Education.*

> The notion that research enhances teaching, a staple argument of those who defend the status quo, is not a compelling justification for the unprofitable marriage (between teaching and research) that now exists. While the exposure to new knowledge and the thoughtful reflexion that accompany research can do much to enliven a teacher, the fact remains that the skills and abilities essential to prolific publication have little to do with good teaching. Good teachers can retain their intellectual vitality without publishing (or at least without publishing much), but professional success as a scholar-researcher depends on substantial publication.
>
> Further, research-based reputations most often are built by intensive work in a very narrow specialty. However, the needs of undergraduates are for introductory-level work, broad exposure to several disciplines, and integrated knowledge. Few undergraduates are ever going to have any extended use for the cutting-edge knowledge of narrow research fields. Their need is principally for more basic knowledge that will be useful in a variety of fields and contexts. This is not the kind of knowledge contained in the average research-journal article, which is why a life spent writing such articles is not a particularly good foundation for excellent teaching.

In spite of ongoing homogenization, there are still differences between institutions and their missions, so no single role can be recommended for all faculty.

Each institution should sharpen its mission and role statements, and then hire faculty who would seem to "be a fit" for their institution.

Radical Recommendations 36–45
Research over Teaching

36. The production of significant research should continue, but the dominance of research over teaching must be altered.

37. **Doctoral programs must prepare graduate students to teach, to develop general curricula, and to advise.**
38. **All four-year institutions must provide in-service programs to improve teaching.**
39. **Reward systems, even in research universities, must be balanced between teaching and research, or skewed toward teaching.**
40. **The requirement for all faculty to be productive publishing researchers must be eliminated. Those who can and wish to produce significant research should be encouraged to do so.**
41. **Teaching loads for faculty no longer required to produce research can be increased. (On many campuses this will be an overwhelming majority of the faculty.)**

    Thus, large classes can be reduced, because faculty will have time to teach additional sections.

    In addition there should be financial savings from increased faculty teaching productivity, which can enable institutions to reduce the costs to students that have been increasing so rapidly.

    Money from the considerable savings can also be used to substantially increase faculty salaries.

The above recommendations are not intended to relieve some faculty of all research responsibilities. All faculty members at four-year institutions who teach have the following responsibilities.

42. **Each should be thoroughly familiar with research terminology and methodology.**
43. **Each should be able to understand, interpret, and apply research results.**
44. **Each should be up to date on research in his or her specialized field, on relevant pedagogy, and on general curriculum development.**
45. **Each should do research, formal or informal, on how students learn in her classes, what difficulties the students have, and what can be done to alleviate their learning difficulties.**

As we have seen, graduate schools emphasize research and ever-narrowing curricula over teaching more broad and interrelated courses in the preparation of future college teachers. And reward systems for those who teach undergraduates is based primarily, if not totally, on research and publishing volume instead of teaching.

We recommend strongly that preparation for teaching of undergraduates should be made a significant part of doctoral programs, and that good teaching and good research should both be able to achieve the top on the reward scale.

TEN

TEACHING

College students are different in many ways from those of several decades ago, but college still looks much like it did several hundred years ago. As has been pointed out earlier, American higher education has been tremendously slow to change since World War II. This has nowhere been more apparent than in the classrooms, where college teachers teach pretty much as they were taught.

In the Wingspread report, Estelle Tanner says "American classrooms, to date, remain remarkably immune to change. In most, the expert (usually male) stands as he always stood, in front of the class, instructing. He has, as usual, on average, an hour to transfer a certain amount of information to the students, who are, as usual, sitting in rows, taking notes on the material presented. At some point during the semester the students will be, as they always have been, tested on the material. At some point after finishing the course, they will have forgotten much of its content, and by graduation much of that particular class experience will be a dim memory. Few would describe this process or environment as one that promotes either the 'connection between knowledge and the zest of life' that Whitehead argues for, or Gardner's 'deep understandings.'"

While the teaching has remained relatively the same there have been vast changes in society, technology, and student demographics.

Yesterday's traditional student—white, male, middle to upper class, recent high school graduate, attends class full-time at a four-year institution, and lives on campus—is today's exception.

Now there are more women than men on campuses, 43 percent are

105

over the age of twenty-five, three hundred thousand are over fifty, 23 percent are minority students, almost 50 percent attend part-time, many hold full-time jobs, and more students live at home or off campus.

It has long been known by experts on teaching and learning that one of the elementary laws of learning is that the building of new comprehension must always start with what the student brings to the teaching situation. Still, the same process continues in the classroom, just as though none of the above change had taken place, and this in spite of the new vast knowledge about teaching and learning and the remarkable developments in educational technology, very few of which are utilized.

Experts say that the technology could change the entire face of higher education, making it much more interesting and stimulating, and providing considerably more active involvement for students in the process.

A few institutions have pioneered in the use of educational technology, and are studying further expanded options. (See Fantastic Fantasy Future in chapter 11.)

Radical Recommendation 46
Educational Technology

Educationists and educational technologists should jointly explore the feasible uses of technology as an essential part of a plan to rejuvenate undergraduate education.

Unfortunately, most teachers still regard themselves as information disseminators. Studies of syllabi and examination questions suggest that most instructors put great emphasis upon the memorization of factual knowledge.

Other studies have shown that the attention span of students during a lecture fluctuates at around fifteen minutes, so in a fifty-minute lecture, students' minds are likely to drift away several times, and retention of what is heard is poor and diminishes rapidly.

Dr. Patricia L. Cross, a teaching-learning expert and former president of the American Association of Higher Education, said: "In a world in which information changes rapidly and where computers outclass the human mind in the storage and retrieval of information, simple transmission of facts for temporary memorization seems misdirected, if not futile."

In *College*, Boyer says that "learning is an active exercise in which the student must play the lead role." This is not describing a student passively listening to a lecture.

Students need to be helped to develop skills of analysis, synthesis, and reasoning. This cannot be done without a factual base, of course, but near-total concern with fact assimilation is futile.

A primary goal of college teaching must be to help the student learn how to learn and how to apply knowledge to life, so that the student can become a self-starting, efficient, and effective learner who will continue to learn throughout his or her entire life.

Concentration on mastery of individual course segments is a disservice to students if faculty do not assist students to see the interrelatedness of knowledge. The same principle applies to faculty and their research.

David L. Featherman, in discussing the teaching of specialized segments of knowledge instead of wholes, says: "How do we both take advantage of our capacity for specialized knowledge and still possess expertise for reassembling the pieces into wholes? Our current institutional practices at the most prolific research universities mitigate against cross-departmental, cross-discipline, cross-college synthesis." And according to Phillip A. Griffiths, real world problems do not fit within individual disciplines. So if we want our graduates to become problem solvers, we must assist them to gain an integrated view of knowledge, and if our universities are to help society solve its problems, faculty must learn to work together as interdisciplinary research teams.

The case for the inadequacy of college teaching has probably been presented too strongly, even unfairly. There are undoubtedly many faculty members who are dedicated teachers who work hard to help students learn. But none can honestly say that the considerable body of knowledge about collegiate teaching and learning is being thoroughly and widely applied by a majority of faculty members. Even many of those doing a good job could likely do better if they applied more of the current knowledge about teaching and learning.

Rejuvenation of our colleges and universities cannot come about without major attention being given to improving college teaching. Two obstacles stand in the way: (1) campus reward systems, and (2) lack of preparation for collegiate teaching.

Obstacle #16
Campus Faculty Reward Systems

At research universities, research productivity is the determining factor in regard to tenure, promotion, and salary-increase decisions. Teaching, faculty say, is a negligible factor. Research dominates in a similar fashion in the reward systems at a great many other four-year institutions.

Radical Recommendation 47–48
Faculty Reward Systems

47. **Research universities need to value teaching on an equal footing with research, and demonstrate this in the campus faculty reward system, as well as in the elimination of very large classes. (See recommendation 36.)**
48. **Other four-year institutions need to value teaching at the very least on an equal footing with research in campus prestige and in the faculty reward system.**

Obstacle #17
Preparation for Collegiate Teaching

College and university teaching is the only major profession for which no preparation is required for the work the teacher will do throughout his or her entire career.

The Ph.D. is the prestige degree in American higher education, and it is the primary qualification for a four-year college teaching position even though it is not a teaching degree.

The Ph.D. student becomes an expert in a continually narrowing field of knowledge and a highly competent researcher, usually primarily on the outer fringe of his or her narrow area of expertise. Such preparation produces some who become national and international authorities in their field, and who produce research of real significance. But it does not prepare them and all the other Ph.D. graduates to be effective teachers of undergraduates.

Over the years there have been many expressions of concern about the lack of preparation of college teachers. In the 1950s, under the sponsorship of the Fund for the Advancement of Education, the Committee of Fifteen (all distinguished educators) studied the critical problems of American graduate schools. Two statements from their report follow: First, "the Ph.D. is not a teaching degree, and it does not certify teaching ability." Second, "there should be established another doctor's degree, not less rigorous, but different. The training designed for this degree should be directed toward preparing men and women to teach effectively in college."

Both Dr. Cross and Dr. Boyer and many others have called for improved preparation in graduate schools for prospective college teachers.

In response to such concerns, a new degree—Doctor of Arts—was established more than three decades ago.

Where the Ph.D. emphasized great depth in a narrowing field, the D.A. provides some depth, but also breadth to enable the teacher of undergraduates to integrate knowledge among fields for students, and to teach interdisciplinary courses.

Where the Ph.D. puts great emphasis on research "on the cutting edge" of a narrow field, the D.A., to a somewhat lesser degree, emphasizes research, primarily in pedagogy. Nevertheless, the Doctor of Arts is under the direction of the major department—English, history, etc.—not the department, school, or college of education.

The D.A. provides study in psychology of human learning, course and curricular development, teaching techniques, use of education technology, tests and measurement, and overview of higher education, plus a supervised teaching internship.

All the suggested pedagogy-related topics can be combined into three or four courses, leaving two-thirds to three-fourths of the required number of course-hours to be taken in the major and related fields.

In an article by Kirby L. Koriath and Margaret Merrion for a 1992 issue of the *Review of Higher Education*, Paul Dressel is quoted as suggesting that in the major and related fields, a few courses could be presented as "integrative, interdisciplinary seminars or problem courses which seek to develop the unifying principles of the several disciplines studied."

In *Scholarship Reconsidered*, Ernest Boyer proposes an altered view of scholarship with components similar to most of those contained in the D.A., but he does not propose a new degree. Rather, he suggests augmentation of the Ph.D. programs. However, many have said that the Ph.D. program is already too long. Adding to its length—courses to provide breadth, courses in pedagogy, and a supervised teaching internship—does not seem feasible.

Also, it seems incongruous to add breadth of subject matter within and even across disciplines to Ph.D. programs, which focus not only on a discipline, but often on a narrow slice within a discipline.

Radical Recommendations 49–53
Improve College Teaching

49. **Develop Doctor of Arts programs to provide graduate students preparation for undergraduate teaching.**
50. **Continue Ph.D. programs for those who wish to pursue a career in research.**

A flow of new D.A. graduates to colleges and universities would not likely begin until three to five years from now. To begin improvement in college teaching sooner, in-service teaching-improvement programs would be needed on campuses across the country. Who would be qualified to head such programs? Possibly no one on many campuses.

Here would be an opportunity for several alert universities to jointly or individually apply to foundations for grants to establish pilot, concentrated, summer teaching-improvement programs on the D.A. pattern.

Some other institutions then could select one or two (a limit should be placed on the number from each school) faculty members, with a strong interest in teaching, and very highly regarded by his or her peers, to participate in the program.

These outstanding faculty then, at the conclusion of the summer program, would return to their own campuses where they would participate in selecting a representative from each department who also would be very interested in teaching and very highly regarded by their departmental peers.

The summer program attendee would then work with the group of elite departmental representatives to help them develop full comprehension of the summer program content as well as the skills attained there. Then each department representative would work with other members of his or her department to help them gain the comprehension and skills needed to improve teaching.

51. **Several universities should seek grants to establish pilot, concentrated, summer, teaching-improvement programs on the D.A. pattern.**
52. **Some other institutions should then send to the summer program one or two of their faculty who have a strong interest in teaching and who are most highly regarded by their peers.**
53. **At the conclusion of the summer program, the attendees should return to their campuses and develop in-service teaching-improvement programs there.**

Obstacle # 18
Distressing Trends

The rapid increase in the proportion of part-time instructors and graduate students used to teach undergraduates in American universities is alarming, as are the suspected two reasons for the increase. Many professors prefer not to teach freshmen and sophomores, and are thereby relieved of an odious chore. And, using part-time instructors and graduate students in the classrooms is a great cost saver for the university.

There also seems to be an increase in assigning teaching responsibilities to persons who are unable to communicate effectively in spoken English.

Radical Recommendation 54
Teaching Assignments

Part-timers and graduate students should be given teaching assignments only if it is ascertained that they will make effective, positive contributions to the instructional program.

ELEVEN

PROBING DEEP INTO TEACHING AND LEARNING— AND WHAT ABOUT THE INTERNET?

T he just completed cursory discussions of the faculty role and college teaching in chapters 9 and 10 provided the basis for the presentation of four obstacles to reform and nineteen radical recommendations.

Since teaching and improvement of learning opportunities for undergraduates are at the heart of this book's recommendations for reform in American higher education, this chapter will present a much more comprehensive and in-depth look at teaching and learning-related topics, ranging from the preparation of teachers, to the lecture, to the Internet.

Improving teaching is one of the most complex and difficult tasks facing reformers for a number of reasons. I have listed twelve of them under various categories. I will cite them first and then discuss them in turn.

Preparation

1. A Ph.D. degree does not prepare a faculty member for teaching.
2. A hiring institution generally does little if anything to prepare the faculty member to teach.

Evaluation

3. Department chairpersons have not been prepared for teaching, for helping faculty members become effective teachers, or for evaluating teaching.
4. A possibility of litigation poses a serious threat to the evaluator.

Academic Freedom

5. A misinterpretation of academic freedom likely intimidates a chairperson and insulates a faculty member in regard to a cooperative effort to improve teaching.

Tenure

6. Tenure provides career-long job protection for a faculty member whose teaching is poor and who makes little effort to improve.

Reward System

7. Campus reward systems often emphasize research and publication, with teaching being a negligible factor in tenure, promotion, and salary decisions.

Other Recognition

8. Nonstudent campus publications often give recognition to faculty for research, publications, presentations at professional meetings, etc., but rarely for effective teaching.

Faculty Hiring

9. In written applications and prehiring interviews, emphasis of the hiring institution is generally on the degrees, research, and publishing of the candidate.

Full-Time Faculty Position

10. There is an increase in the long-time use of graduate students (teaching assistants) to teach undergraduate classes (primarily freshmen) at institutions with extensive graduate programs.

11. As financial exigency becomes more extreme in colleges and universities, more "taxicab" instructors—part-time adjuncts—are hired for modest stipends.

Class Sizes

12. Financial exigency often leads to significantly increased class sizes.

In the following discussion, suggestions will be made for dealing with the just-enumerated twelve difficulties presented to those who would improve college and university teaching.

PREPARATION: THE PH.D.

Reason One: Graduate schools generally ignore teacher preparation. Many experts for a great many years have decried the lack of adequate preparation for college teachers. In the mid-1950s under the sponsorship of the Fund for the Advancement of Education, the Committee of Fifteen (very distinguished educators) studied the then-critical problems of American graduate schools. Three statements from their report follow:

First, the Ph.D. is not a teaching degree, and it does not certify teaching ability.

Second, "In our national effort of one hundred years ago to bring American scholarship up to European standards, it was right to lay special emphasis upon training in research. But by so doing, the problems of teaching were neglected."

Third, "There should be established another doctor's degree, not less rigorous, but different. The training designed for this degree should be directed toward preparing men and women to teach effectively in college. It should emphasize the breadth of the candidate's knowledge and the clarity of his understanding."

As was stated in chapter 3, the Ph.D. student becomes an expert in a continually narrowing field of knowledge, and she becomes a highly competent researcher, usually primarily on the outer fringe of her narrow area of expertise. Such preparation produces some who become national and international authorities in their field, and who produce research of real significance. But it does not prepare them and all the other Ph.D. graduates to be effective teachers of undergraduates.

Occasionally there have been ripples of concern about the preparation of college teachers. Some universities have provided a quick primer on college teaching for their teaching assistants who are also Ph.D. candidates. And in 1993 a project called Preparing Future Faculty was sponsored by the Association of American Colleges and Universities and the Council of Graduate Schools. Seventeen Ph.D.-awarding universities participated in the program funded by a three-year grant of $1.8 million. Some other universities have started similar projects.

In the PFF project, mentor programs have been created, and a participating university had to establish partnerships with colleges that emphasize teaching. A February 1996 *Chronicle of Higher Education* article said of the PFF project: "the new efforts are an intensive introduction to curriculum development, the service duties of professors, and the workload that they face at different types of institutions. . . . They offer monthly seminars on such topics as shared governance, academic freedom, and getting the first job." But what about what constitutes effective teaching?

The article continues: "Persuading some professors to support the PFF program is not easy. . . . Some professors view it as a 'distraction' from a student's graduate course work and research." This entrenched lack of concern about teaching may make it difficult to alter Ph.D. programs to provide a significant teaching component, but it is encouraging to see that some are recognizing the need for such a component.

An alternative to the Ph.D.—the Doctor of Arts degree—was discussed in an article by Kirby L. Koriath and Margaret M. Merrion in the fall 1992 issue of the *Review of Higher Education*.

> In the 1960s, after decades of discussion centering on whether the Ph.D. was a suitable credential for undergraduate teaching, plans for a new doctoral program emerged. Paul Dressel and Frances Delisle suggested that a degree for preparing college teachers should contain four elements:
>
>   (1) Content courses in one or more disciplines, with integrative, interdisciplinary seminars or problem courses which seek to develop the unifying principles of the several disciplines studied;
>   (2) Seminars for developing the professional knowledge and skills required in instruction, curriculum development, evaluation;

(3) Individual problems courses developing research methodology and integrative scholarly skills relevant to instruction; and

(4) Internships involving two or three stages of increasing instructional and curricular responsibility.

The article continues that the above components—broad disciplinary and interdisciplinary studies, formal course work in pedagogy, and curriculum-based teaching apprenticeships—became the cornerstone of the new Doctor of Arts degree.

Koriath and Merrion conclude that "over twenty years ago, with notable clairvoyance, those who created offered, and supervised this degree [D.A.] anticipated and attempted to address many of the shortcomings which then were, and today still are, laid at the feet of traditional doctoral education [Ph.D.]."

Describing the D.A., the Council of Graduate Schools in the United States says:

[The Doctor of Arts degree purports to prepare] professional, academically well-qualified teaching scholars for college classrooms. . . . [In contradistinction to the Ph.D., the goal of the D.A. is to] produce broad competence in contrast with research specialization. . . . The purpose is to provide integration of knowledge for undergraduate teaching, not to specialize and fragment what the teaching scholar knows and learns. . . . [Within the student's major,] interdepartmental and interdisciplinary study are desirable. . . . Course selection should thus be typically broader and less narrowly specialized than for the Ph.D. and may bridge several supportive disciplines. . . . [The D.A. graduate will have the ability] to integrate and synthesize, to compare data and information, and to apply knowledge. . . . [The D.A. program will include] carefully supervised teaching experiences. These should include full responsibility for teaching courses, the mentorship of experienced professors, and other experiences including courses and/or seminars in the structure and problems of higher education. . . . [The D.A.] must provide for the development of research skills so that the teaching scholar can maintain the quality of his own scholarship and can utilize the results of research in the classroom.

[The dissertation or project] may take several acceptable forms. The evaluation and synthesis of academic or disciplinary knowledge, comparative studies, creative intellectual projects, expository dissertations, or significant research in teaching problems and the organization of new concepts of course work are applicable.

Dr. Fred Harcleroad (former university president, former president of the American College Testing Program, and later director of the Center for the Study of Higher Education at the University of Arizona) overoptimistically said in 1972 that the D.A. "may be the most significant step toward improving college teaching in a century and may well be one of the great historical contributions of higher education in the United States." Dr. Harcleroad made this statement after he had served as an evaluative consultant for the Tennessee Higher Education Commission on the fledgling Doctor of Arts program at Middle Tennessee State University.

Unfortunately this prediction has not yet been fulfilled. Only twenty-one universities have D.A. programs, producing a very small number of graduates, compared to the overwhelming number of Ph.D. recipients.

There are probably a number of reasons for the lack of widespread development of D.A. programs, but the fact remains that the Ph.D. dominates all of American higher education, and it is the degree of prestige. Whether the Doctor of Arts achieves its great potential will depend on whether administrators, faculty, and governing boards defy the Ph.D. dominance and place the effective learning of undergraduates above the Ph.D. prestige factor.

If undergraduates are to be well served, the Doctor of Arts will likely be the teaching degree of the future, with prestige equal to that now enjoyed by the Ph.D.

Hiring Institutions

Reason Two: Hiring institutions need to have in-service programs to assist faculty to achieve excellence in teaching. Institutional goals for student learning need to be continually stressed; instructional development expertise should be made available to faculty, as should education technology, and production of education materials.

EVALUATION: DEPARTMENT CHAIRPERSONS

Reason Three: Department chairpersons must be experts on teaching and learning if they are to effectively perform their supervisory responsibilities of (a) guiding faculty toward teaching excellence, and (b) evaluating an individual faculty member's teaching. The latter is essential if reward systems are to be altered to emphasize teaching on at least a par with research.

In response to his 1990 book *Scholarship Reconsidered*, in which he suggested the broadening of the description of scholarship to include teaching and service, Ernest Boyer received many calls on how to evaluate faculty work in all its forms. The responses were summarized in a February 9, 1994, article in the *Chronicle of Higher Education* as follows: "Without clear and widely accepted standards for assessing teaching and service, their status will never receive the same respect given to a scholar's research and publications."

Such standards cannot be developed, let alone accepted, until faculty and academic administrators—especially chairpersons—are knowledgeable about learning and teaching theory and practice.

Evaluation of teaching is especially difficult. A sound approach might be as follows: The department chairperson, who is thoroughly prepared in teaching and learning, will have conferences with each faculty member at the beginning of the course and the end of the course. These conferences will stress institution goals, course goals, means of achieving each goal, and specific means for assessing student progress toward achievement of the goals. Each instructor will be responsible for the development of course plans and for providing evidence of the success of the students in achieving the goals.

Student evaluation on the specific goals, means, and testing should be used. Some form of peer evaluation may also be useful when faculty are well schooled on teaching and learning.

Litigation

Reason Four: The responsibility of developing the course plan and of providing evidence of its success should be the instructor's, to lessen the *possibility of litigation* against the evaluator and the institution, and to avoid the appearance of violation of the academic freedom of the faculty member.

ACADEMIC FREEDOM

Reason Five: Colleges and universities must be more discriminating in their interpretation of academic freedom. Many faculty would wrap academic freedom around themselves like a protective cloak to insulate themselves from any scrutiny of their activities.

Some years ago at a private college, one of the best teachers on the campus and the college dean, who shared a good personal relationship, were discussing improving teaching on the campus. At one point the teacher said, "If you were to enter my classroom during a class, I would stop teaching until you left."

This incident is presented here, not to indicate that administrators should visit classes in progress, but rather to demonstrate the attitude, apparently shared by a great many faculty and sometimes espoused by the American Association of University Professors, that administrators should not "intrude" in the "faculty domain"—the academic program.

Academic administrators—department chairpersons, deans, and vice presidents—are not sinister invaders from another planet. They have virtually all been professors, that is, teachers and researchers, and faculty colleagues, who now share a broader responsibility for the effectiveness of the performance of the institution's basic functions—teaching, research, and public service.

A department chair, knowledgeable about teaching and learning and assisting individual faculty members to continually seek ways to facilitate more and better student learning, is not violating the faculty member's academic freedom. Rather, this is a cooperative effort on the part of the chairperson and the faculty member to discharge their joint responsibility to provide the students with the maximum in learning opportunities. To do less would be unfair to the student.

What more logically constitutes a threat to academic freedom is the current obsession with political correctness. An example of a real threat to academic freedom would be a situation in which a faculty member, because of pressures from any source, would be dissuaded from doing legitimate research on possible mental and physical differences among races, and/or discussing such research in the classroom.

A college or university must be a place where ideas can vie in open combat for the minds of men and women in the classroom and elsewhere on the campus.

TENURE

Reason Six: Because of the protection by the courts now afforded to faculty, tenure is not nearly as important as it was many years ago, when a newly elected governor might replace many of the faculty at a state institution with some of his supporters.

In order to give an institution more leverage to encourage faculty members to continually strive to improve their performance rather than to slack off once tenure has been awarded, it may be time to consider a time-limitation type of tenure. Tenure might be awarded for a specific number of years—possibly seven—after which the faculty member would be reevaluated for the possible awarding of tenure for another specified number of years.

REWARD SYSTEMS

Reason Seven: The blame for campus reward systems that emphasize research over teaching should not be laid at the feet of faculty. Actually, according to surveys by Boyer and others, a great many faculty members would respond with enthusiasm and give more time to the teaching process if campus reward systems were altered to emphasize teaching at least on a par with research.

OTHER RECOGNITION

Reason Eight: Several awards of several thousand dollars each should be provided each year to those teachers selected as the best that year. The awards might be presented at a dinner or a special assembly at which other outstanding teachers would be recognized also.

A number of smaller awards—possibly $500 each—might be provided during the year to teachers who exhibit creativity and pedagogical knowledge in redesigning a course or courses to be more interesting, stimulating, and effective.

A periodic campus newsletter could deal with some interesting things some teachers are doing to improve student learning. Such a publication would not only give recognition to innovative teachers, but likely also would stimulate others to be creative.

Also, the public relations staff should seek out interesting instructional techniques throughout the year which are being used on the campus, and provide feature stories and pictures to the off-campus media—local, state, regional, and national.

FACULTY HIRING: A CANDIDATE'S EMPHASIS

Reason Nine: If you (as an institution) were to hire a Doctor of Arts graduate into a department that had a chairperson who was well prepared to stimulate good teaching and evaluate it, and you had a reward and recognition system emphasizing teaching, you still might get poor or mediocre teaching if your new teacher was not really enthusiastic about teaching.

In hiring interviews, the reasons a candidate is applying for a faculty position should be explored. Does he like students and enjoy working with them; is she enthusiastic about her field of expertise, and about relating knowledge in her field to other fields?

Does he get real satisfaction and even excitement from helping students learn and seeing them grow into skilled, maturing learners?

Hiring Graduate Students

Reason Ten: As discussed in chapter 3, in a *60 Minutes* segment in 1995, Lesley Stahl reported that all 150 freshman English classes at the University of Arizona were taught by graduate students, and the only time freshmen saw real professors was in huge lecture classes. This is a common practice in American universities.

The benefit to the universities is that using graduate assistants to teach courses that would otherwise be taught by a tenured professor can save the institution two-thirds to three-fourths the cost of each professor so replaced.

Disadvantages to students are:

1. The teaching assistant likely has had no formal preparation for college teaching and little if any college teaching experience.
2. The T.A.'s primary concern is her graduate program, and she is understandably going to concentrate most of her time and effort on graduate studies rather than on teaching freshmen.
3. American graduate schools attract bright students from around the world, some of whom become teaching assistants. Many, especially in the sciences and mathematics, can barely speak English, and freshmen, therefore, have great difficulty understanding them.

Teaching assistants should be provided with formal preparation for college teaching and supervision by experienced professors.

Graduate course loads of T.A.s should be limited so they can devote sufficient time to their concurrent teaching responsibilities.

Professors are sometimes hired because of their research skills, even though they cannot effectively communicate orally in the English language. Putting such professors and similarly handicapped T.A.s in the classroom is a total affront to undergraduates and illustrates the ultimate in lack of concern for its undergraduates by a university.

No one should be permitted to teach who cannot communicate effectively with students.

The use of teaching assistants to do most of the teaching of freshmen flies right in the face of student retention experts who say that the critical period for retention of students is the first six weeks of the freshman year, and that the best teachers should teach freshmen at the outset.

Ms. Stahl reported in her *60 Minutes* interview story that at the University of Arizona freshmen are taught by graduate students or part-timers 87 percent of the time.

In Florida at public universities, 60 percent of lower-division undergraduate courses are taught by nontenure-track faculty members, many of whom are part-timers.

Part-Timers

Reason Eleven: The proportion of *part-time faculty* members in the United States has been increasing steadily, and stood at about 41 percent nationally for teaching faculty members, according to a 1995 study by David Leslie and Judith Gappa.

Part-time faculty members are paid small stipends (a great deal less than full-time faculty) and they receive no health or pension benefits, all of which saves considerable amounts of money for universities. And part-timers often don't receive offices or other institutional support. This low-cost instruction benefits the university budget.

But what about student benefit? There can be some if the part-time instructor has direct and current experience in the field in which he is teaching, as such a teacher can bring up-to-date information and current illustrations to the classroom.

There is, however, a significant downside. Part-time teachers seldom are paid for office hours, so they are often unavailable to students for guidance outside the classroom. Nor are they compensated for committee work or the myriad of other activities that make a university function, so few tend to be involved.

Part-time faculty should not be hired because they provide low-cost instruction, but rather because they have unique and effective contributions to make to student learning. And such "taxicab professors" should be compensated for making themselves available to students outside the classroom on a regular basis.

CLASS SIZE

Reason Twelve: Classes of several hundred up to one thousand or more cannot be taught; they can only be addressed. No large classes should be used without providing for interaction between instructor and students through some means such as the inclusion of small discussion sections in the course plan along with large lecture sections, or the use of an electronic learning response system in conjunction with large lecture sessions (as described later in this chapter).

CRITICISMS OF UNDERGRADUATE INSTRUCTION STILL AROUND

"Using talented manpower as 'talking books' is a shameful waste in most of our colleges and universities today, and tends to keep the student a permanent adolescent. The student's umbilical cord must be severed at graduation in any event, and we should take the responsibility of playing midwife at an earlier stage."

This colorful statement was taken from the 1967 report of the distinguished Committee on Undergraduate Teaching sponsored by the Hazen Foundation. Over a period of three years the committee and its staff gathered and deliberated on the voluminous and growing literature on learning and teaching and experimentation in college teaching. The committee's statement would seem to have some validity today.

In spite of all the criticism of undergraduate instruction and all the recommendations for improvement prior to the late 1960s (when the Doctor of Arts concept first appeared); and more than thirty years after the introduction of the first D.A. programs, there is a vast amount of evidence that a great need for improvement in college teaching still exists.

This is not due to the failure of the D.A. concept, but rather in part (1) to the prestige power of the Ph.D., which has kept the D.A. from being widely accepted, and (2) the reluctance of higher education to accept change.

Undergraduate education was strongly criticized in the middle and late 1980s and the early 1990s by such prestigious groups as the American Association of Colleges, the National Institute of Education, The National Endowment for the Humanities, and the Carnegie Foundation for the Advancement for Teaching (see chapter 4). These organizations all reported similar and very sobering information, and prescribed strong recommendations for improvement.

Dr. Ernest Boyer says in *College* (the report of the Carnegie study), that in the mid-1980s, the lecture method was preferred by most professors.

Boyer quotes Mortimer Adler as saying ". . . all genuine learning is active, not passive. It involves the use of the mind, not just memory. It is a process of discovery in which the student is the main agent, not the teacher."

Boyer continues, "In all too many classrooms, we found an absence of intellectual exchange. . . ."

The NIE report says, "Faculty should make great use of active modes of teaching and require that students take greater responsibility for their learning."

THE LECTURE EXAMINED

The recommendation for active modes of teaching and criticisms of the lecture in this book should not be interpreted as a total condemnation of the use of lecture in college teaching. What is being criticized is the sole or predominate use of the lecture method throughout a course without regard to its effectiveness in promoting student learning.

Selective use of the lecture along with the use of techniques to minimize the deficiencies of the lecture as a teaching mode can make the lecture a valuable option for the pedagogically knowledgeable faculty member.

Dr. William J. McKeachie, then-director for the Center for Research on Learning and Teaching at the University of Michigan, said about the lecture in *New Directions for Teaching and Learning* in 1980:

We do not need to lecture when concepts are available in printed form at an appropriate level for our students. In general, print presents information in a form which can be covered more rapidly and in a way more accessible for retrieval than lectures. Students using printed materials can choose their own rate of learning: they can review, they can skip, they can vary the order. The lecturer thus starts with some serious handicaps; however, not all information is available in printed form. For example, most printed sources available to college and university teachers for assignment to students are at least several years out of date by the time they are available for assignments.

Lectures are particularly appropriate for helping students get up-to-date information on current research and theories relevant to topics they are studying. Moreover, lectures may sometimes usefully summarize material scattered over a variety of printed sources, thus providing a more efficient method of conveying information than if students were to be assigned to cover these sources by their own reading. Finally, a lecturer can adapt material to the background and interests of a particular audience—material which in printed form is at a level or in a style not well suited to a particular class. . . . [A]ppropriate lectures can build structures and expectations that help students read material in the given subject-matter area more effectively.

Many lectures have important motivational functions. By helping students become aware of the problem, of conflicting points of view, or of challenges to ideas they have previously taken for granted, the lecturer can stimulate interest in further learning in an area. Moreover, the lecturer's own attitudes and enthusiasm have an important effect upon student motivation.

So, selecting the reasons for using a lecture is most important. If another mode of instruction can more efficiently and effectively stimulate the desired student learning at that point, then likely the lecture should not be used. Thus, the lecture should be used occasionally in a course when it is the most appropriate method to achieve specific goals. But, use of the lecture indiscriminately throughout a course is what lecture critics deplore.

How the lecture is used is just as important as why it is used. In *New Directions for Teaching and Learning*, McKeachie writes "[T]he organization of the lecture needs to take account of the students' existing knowledge and expectations. . . . [S]tudents' information processing capacities are limited, and a lecturer who is an expert in the field is likely to overestimate the students' ability to grasp large blocks of material and to see relationships . . . thus lecturers often overload the students' capacity so they become less able to understand than if fewer points had been presented." Instead of a continuous, uninterrupted presentation, McKeachie points out that students could learn better from a lecture "if there were periodic summaries of preceding material." Occasionally the instructor should raise "specific questions that will test the students' understanding. . . . Pointing out relationships, asking rhetorical questions, or asking questions to be answered by class members are ways of encouraging active thought." And, the lecturer should always keep in mind the Hartley and Davies findings that: ". . . typically, attention increases from the beginning of the lecture to ten minutes into the lecture and decreases after that point. One evidence of this was after the lecture, students recalled 70 percent of the material covered in the first ten minutes, and only 20 percent of the material covered in the last ten minutes."

OTHER WAYS TO ENLIVEN INSTRUCTION

In his 1962 work titled *The American College and Its Teachers*, F. C. Rosecrance alleges that 85 percent of the average person's learning comes through sight rather than through hearing.

Whether that percentage is accurate or not, there can be no denying that we and entering college students have been bombarded by the visual through the mass media for most of our lives, especially since the advent of television. We are conditioned to the visual, and to spend many hours in a classroom where the visual is not a factor can be stultifying to the student.

The Committee on Undergraduate Teaching says that a teacher in almost any field should seek out experienced advice on how to improve the quality of conceptual learning by combining both visual and verbal presentations.

In his 1980 work titled *Surviving the Eighties*, Lewis Mayhew said that technology had created many electronic, mechanical, and audiovisual devices to assist teachers, and that they must be taught to utilize the newer media. Technical dexterity, he explained, is important, but even more significant is awareness of how to use devices for the achievement of educational objectives.

And apparently few faculty are taking full advantage of the potential stimulus of media in the classroom. The AAC report says, "No faculty has fully exploited the technological developments—film, video, computer—that will ease the burden of making their courses as widely effective as our minimum required curriculum would allow."

SPECIALIZATION

Clark Kerr says in *Higher Education Cannot Escape History* (1994), that the internationalization of learning has intensified specialization, particularly in research, and by extension into teaching. Kerr writes:

> Larger worldwide communities of specialists mean that specialists write increasingly for each other and less and less for wide readership within their disciplines and related fields of knowledge. More and more specialties have a critical mass of scholars that subsist within their own confines. They have their own vast literature to read and large num-

bers of colleagues to know, and are driven to seek smaller and smaller topics to explore in the effort to gain recognition. Internationalization of learning means also the further fractionalization of knowledge. . . .

Then there is the intense specialization in doctoral programs that leads to narrow specialization in undergraduate courses.

In *College*, Boyer says: "The disciplines have fragmented themselves into smaller and smaller pieces, and undergraduates find it difficult to see patterns in their courses and to relate what they learn to life. . . . We found a longing among undergraduates for a more coherent view of knowledge."

As the AAC report points out, "Real life is interdisciplinary," and the graduate preparation of faculty should enable undergraduate teachers to transcend discipline lines and help students to interrelate knowledge.

FACULTY PREPARATION

Concerning the preparation of undergraduate faculty, the AAC report says: "The Ph.D. candidate should be introduced in a systematic way to the profession of teaching. The qualifying process should include acquaintance with the literature on human learning and evaluation as well as apprentice teaching, subject to peer observation and the criticism of veteran teachers. The candidate should demonstrate competence in designing a syllabus and examinations, and selecting textbooks, readings, and laboratory materials."

The NIE report says: "We are concerned that the graduate education of those doctoral students who do intend to teach in colleges and universities include some exposure to the requirements of effective undergraduate teaching and learning."

Dr. K. Patricia Cross, former research psychologist at the Center for Research and Development in Higher Education at the University of California at Berkeley, and more recently of Harvard University, is a longtime student of college teaching and learning, as evinced by her book *Accent on Learning*, and by her articles and speeches. In the 1980s she was one of the most noteworthy spokespersons for improving college teaching, having made her case before thousands of educators at AAHE national meetings, as well as in articles in the *AAHE Bulletin*. She served as president of AAHE in 1985.

In "A Proposal to Improve Teaching" in a 1986 *AAHE Bulletin*, Dr. Cross makes reference to quotes from the AAC, NIE, and Carnegie studies as well as other research on teaching and learning. The following are some quotations from the article:

> Lecturing students has long been decried, yet it is the overwhelming method of choice for college teachers. On any measure of efficiency, the lecture is a very ineffective way to get people to know subject matter.
>
> . . . [T]he purpose of disseminating information while most common, is also the least useful. In a world in which information changes rapidly and where computers outclass the human mind in the storage and retrieval of information, simple transmission of facts for temporary memorization seems misdirected, if not futile.
>
> The research shows that most teachers regard themselves as information disseminators.
>
> There is some danger that students in our classrooms are drowning in information. Many of their teachers teach as they were taught. There is nothing in their preparation and training to break the cycle of teaching as telling.

According to Cross, Astin says that the major goal of undergraduate teaching is to get students intellectually involved, and Cross adds, ". . . to get every student actively involved in the work of the class and with one another."

She continues:

> We need more research on techniques that teachers can use that will induce in students the productive involvement with worthwhile goals that makes a difference in their lives.
>
> In this era of knowledge explosion, what students know when they leave college will not be nearly as important as what they are capable of learning.
>
> . . . [T]he needs of the 21st Century are for broadly educated people who can and will use their minds to invent new products or procedures and who can interpret trends or analyze problems.
>
> Ideas are far more important to our world than information.
>
> I really think the graduate school has to take an enormous amount of blame for doing nothing to prepare people for what they're going to spend their professional lives doing (teaching).
>
> . . . [A]fter hiring, more needs to be done to help faculty continue to improve and assess their teaching.

She points to the graduate schools, saying that they should take on the responsibility for developing and teaching the methodological tools for classroom research, so that classroom teachers would have the research skills to measure the impact of their teaching on student learning.

The AAC report discusses pedagogical research that could be done in a new kind of doctoral program, or by faculty teaching in a discipline. The AAC report says:

> A new area of research, still in its infancy, has been evolving during the last decade. It arose and is still rooted in the natural sciences. It is directed toward understanding how students learn (or fail to learn) specific subject matter, what difficulties they have with various modes of abstract logical reasoning, what preconceptions or misconceptions impede their mastery of concepts or principles in the given subject, what instructional approaches and devices are effective in helping learners overcome the obstacles which are encountered, what exercises and feedback accelerate the development of various desirable skills, and how best to make use of new instructional technology. . . .
>
> We refer . . . to research indigenous to specific subject areas, such as physics—research having results that can be readily understood and directly applied by teachers of the subject. Such research could and should be conducted in disciplines other than the natural sciences, and wide application of the insights thus gained into teaching and learning could have a dramatic impact on all of undergraduate education.

In *Scholarship Reconsidered: Priorities of the Professoriate*, Ernest Boyer argues that "doctoral study will contribute effectively toward shaping the 'new scholar' when it contains six components: specialized study with original research, interdisciplinary course work that promotes breadth of understanding, a flexible dissertation requirement, applied scholarship incorporating field experiences and practice or apprenticeships, preparation for teaching that is curriculum-based, and a mentoring relationship with a master teacher."

A New Doctor's Degree

The following story about a university's unique thrust in the early 1970s for teaching excellence is true, but the institution will not be identified.

A state college had just recently been granted university status by the state's legislature. Shortly thereafter the state established a commission to coordinate state higher education. One of the first responsibilities of the commission was to develop a master plan for each state institution, and combine those plans into a master plan for the state.

A new president from out of state had recently come to the newly established university. When guidelines for initial planning were sent by the commission to each institution, the new president saw the opportunity to hasten the institution's development from a college to a university by expanding its academic offerings both horizontally and vertically, and by increasing its emphasis on research and public services.

The president urged the faculty to explore the expansion of academic programs horizontally with the possible addition of programs at the bachelor's and master's levels and vertically into doctoral programs.

The state—relatively small in population—had two universities offering Ph.D. programs, but no regional university offered doctoral programs.

The president understood that the state's limited financial resources would make it impossible for the state to permit a proliferation of Ph.D. programs at the regional universities. Still, he had learned much about good college teaching in his own doctoral program and he felt strongly about the need to provide professors with the tools they needed to be highly effective teachers of undergraduates.

The more he thought about it, preparing doctoral students for college teaching seemed to be in perfect harmony with the institution's historic teacher-preparation role. The institution was initially established as a two-year normal school for the preparation of teachers. Next it became a four-year teacher's college, primarily for the preparation of teachers. During the successive evolution to a state college and then in the early days as a regional university, the preparation of teachers was still a primary function.

What a logical step, then, to extend the institution's function from the preparation of teachers for kindergarten through high school to include the preparation of teachers for colleges.

About this time the president heard E. Alden Dunham present the new Doctor of Arts concept at a national higher education meeting. The Doctor of Arts seemed perfect for his university and for the preparation of teachers of undergraduates. He immediately set out to rough out a D.A. proposal with the assistance of the dean of the graduate school, who was the only other person on campus with a doctor's degree in higher education. Because of the deadline on campus master plans, there was not time for full consultation on campus.

While the overview of the D.A. concept was presented to the governing board and the coordinating commission, faculty on the campus in several disciplines worked hard to develop the specifics of D.A. programs in their departments.

The governing board approved the programs. The coordinating commission had announced that there would be no doctoral programs approved for any of the regional universities, but they became so intrigued by the Doctor of Arts concept that they gave provisional approval to the D.A. programs.

Because the state was in a financial "crunch," the commission had determined that there would be no additional money provided for new programs, and that no new programs could be begun unless an institution could show that it had the necessary "start-up" money.

The commission and the university came to agreement on what beginning the D.A. program would cost, and the university did not have the money. The president and the university foundation launched a drive for the funds—a considerable sum for a fledgling university—and the goal was quickly reached. Then the commission approved the program.

A Learning Resource Center

The president had developed a fascination with learning resource centers—a relatively new development in higher education. He visualized a learning resource center on the campus to complement the Doctor of Arts program.

He wanted to provide D.A. students with the utmost in educational technology and trained instructional experts to aid the students in doing pedagogical experimentation and research.

He wanted to provide the faculty with educational technology, instructional expert assistance, and production personnel to enable a good teaching faculty to become a great teaching faculty.

He reasoned that if the university was going to produce D.A. graduates who would exemplify the best in current, effective, college teaching techniques, then surely the university faculty should do the same.

Instead of attempting to guide the university in a hopeless quest to emulate research universities, which at best would produce a struggling fourth- or fifth-rate imitation of the prestige research institutions, he hoped to see the embryonic university stress its initial mission and become an institution that did some research but was focused on becoming the best teaching institution in the region and beyond.

He had done some reading on learning resource centers, he had attended a weeklong workshop on educational technology at Ohio State University, and he had learned about the learning response system at a meeting of the American Association of Higher Education in Chicago. And he had also become aware of two outstanding, very new learning resource centers—one at Oral Roberts University, and the other at Central Christian College in Oklahoma.

Once the general concept of a learning resources center was developed and approval was given by the governing board, he planned several exploratory trips.

The president, the campus planner, and the architect visited Oral Roberts and Central Christian College where they saw some of the newest educational technology in use. Next, they flew to New York, where at the Rochester Institute of Technology they saw a great deal of technology in use. What was relevant and feasible they included in the university Learning Resource Plan, along with the learning response system.

Some of the major components of the university's finished learning resource center were:

1. A personalized learning laboratory featuring two hundred carrels, equipped with television sets, filmstrip projectors, tape playback units, etc.
2. A materials development center for the preparation of teaching materials such as charts, graphs, illustrations, videos, photographs, art work, and overhead transparencies.
3. An instructional development center in which staff experts were available to provide assistance to faculty in planning and developing courses.
4. A television and video production center.
5. A multi-media presentation room featuring the unique *learning*

response system. The room provided tiered seating for about four hundred students.

The learning response system functioned as follows:

A professor would prepare a lecture for a fifty-minute class, during which he would plan to make possibly four to six major points. After he had presented the first point or concept, he would push a button at the console at the front of the room, and on a screen behind him on the left, a question would appear which went to the heart of the point he had just presented. The instructor would then press another button, and five potential answers to the question would appear on the screen behind the instructor on the right.

At each student station there were five buttons, and each student would be asked to press the button she thought identified the correct answer. In a few seconds the instructor would have a percentage tabulation of correct answers at the instructor's console. If only 50 percent answered correctly, the instructor knew he needed to try again with perhaps a different approach. The goal was to achieve 100 percent of student comprehension, or close to it.

Interface with the university computer center would enable the instructor to identify students having comprehension difficulties, and the instructor could then provide them with special help.

Although large classes would be served in the multi-media presentation room, feedback and a substantial measure of personalization would be afforded with the use of the learning response system, vastly improving student learning over the traditional large lecture process.

With the Doctor of Arts program and the learning resource center (LRC) on the campus of what had historically been a teaching institution, the president saw the possibility that the university could become a leader in effective college teaching in that region and beyond.

To maximize the potential of the D.A. and the LRC, the president hired Dr. Nevitt Sanford, an eminent human-learning psychologist, as a consultant. Dr. Sanford had recently published *The American College*, a book dealing with many aspects of higher education, which many considered the virtual bible for American educators at that time.

Dr. Sanford came to the campus and discussed a possible grant proposal with faculty and administrators, and provided good advice.

What the president hoped for was a large four- or five-year grant to achieve two goals: First, he wanted funds to enable the university to put a segment of its faculty on a half-time teaching load for one semester, when they would spend half their time with instructional experts in the LRC, replanning all their courses to include the most effective teaching approaches and considerable use of education technology. Each semester a different group of faculty would be given the load reduction for training and course replanning in appropriate teaching techniques and use of technology.

Grant money would be used to provide additional instructional experts and course materials, as well as providing temporary teachers to replace the time of those involved in the teaching-improvement project.

Second, he wanted funds to enable D.A. students and other faculty to do pedagogical experiments and research in the LRC and with LRC personnel.

Unfortunately, the university was not able to develop a grant proposal that was powerful enough to attract the kind of foundation support it was seeking.

The Doctor of Arts and the learning resources center, while making some contributions to effective college teaching, fell far short of achieving the president's lofty aims. He wanted the university, in harmony with its initial mission of teacher preparation, to (1) be a leader in research and experimentation in college teaching; (2) be recognized as one of the most successful teaching institutions in the region, or anywhere; and (3) provide academe with D.A. graduates, each well prepared to perform effectively as teacher, adviser to students, researcher and scholar, curriculum developer, and participant in university policy development and decision making.

He still feels that the ideas and goals were excellent. However, he says that he failed miserably in trying to sell the D.A. and the LRC concepts on campus. He explains that he simply was not able to generate enough support to make major strides toward the goals. And, no wonder!

As he now sees it, he came as an outsider president to the campus. In an early speech to the faculty he stated three major goals: to provide an honors program for outstanding students; to provide remedial programs for those who needed remediation; and to provide improved instruction for all students.

Then came his campaigns for the D.A. and the LRC. Since he kept hammering on improved teaching, he says it is quite likely that many faculty were hurt and angry at what they perceived as a continual denigration of their teaching abilities and performance.

He feels sure that he did not state clearly and often enough that he thought there was much good teaching being done at the university, but that he felt that most teachers (if not all) at the university and at other colleges and universities could improve their performance if they were provided with current knowledge about effective teaching and educational technology (which they had not received in their Ph.D. or other graduate programs), and the services of the LRC and its staff.

A noble experiment was tried, but it did not succeed because of the overzealousness and overinvolvement of the president, and because he didn't take the time with individuals and small groups (1) to thoroughly explain his ideas and goals to administrators and faculty; (2) to seek input and advice from both groups; and (3) to enlist enthusiastic assistance from the highly respected campus leaders—faculty and administration—to help win the support of the rest of the campus.

In view of the Wingspread and the Boyer Commission thrusts for the regeneration of undergraduate education, could it be time for more "noble experiments"?

FANTASTIC FANTASY FUTURE

Nearly a half century ago, some visionaries were predicting a brilliant future for educational technology. And as early as the late 1950s there were indications of some strong interest in developing educational technology for higher education.

By the 1970s there was expanding use of technology in administration, libraries, and research, and information technology for instruction was being heavily used in the military and in-plant training in industry. But in higher education, the use of instructional technology lagged behind.

The Carnegie Commission on Higher Education did a thorough study on instructional technology in higher education in 1972 and produced a report and recommendations in *The Fourth Revolution*.

The commission reported that faculty tend to be resistant or apathetic toward instructional technology. Faculty themselves rate resistance of faculty as second only to lack of funds as the most severe obstacle to the adoption of the new technologies, as reported by Jarrod W. Wilcox in a 1972 MIT study.

The commission's report continues ". . . still, some of the most impressive progress in instructional technology has been inspired by the initiative of individual faculty members who have grasped the potentials of new techniques and have applied them intelligently to their own teaching."

An example was provided by Professor Postlethwait at Purdue University in an individual learning laboratory in the sciences. The laboratories utilized "listening to explanations and instructions on tape; reading assignments in textbooks; use of films, slides, and other visuals; as well as student-conducted experiments guided by instruction sheets and tapes." The results over a several-year period were superior when compared to results of more traditional teaching.

In addition to its effectiveness, the commission predicted that "the new informational technology will eventually (but not necessarily initially) reduce instructional costs below levels possible using conventional methods alone." It made a strong recommendation for the use of instructioal technology. "Because expanding technology will extend higher learning to higher numbers of people who have been unable to take advantage of it in the past, because it will provide instruction in forms that will be more effective than conventional instruction for some learners in some subjects, because it will be more effective for all learners and many teachers under many circumstances, and because it will significantly reduce costs of higher education in the long run, its early advancement should be encouraged by the adequate commitment of colleges and universities to its utilization and development and by adequate support from governmental and other agencies concerned with the advancement of higher learning."

A somewhat "fantasy future" was predicted by the commission: ". . . by the year 2000 it now appears that a significant proportion of instruction in higher education on campus may be carried on through informational technology. . . ." By the year 2000, "all instructional technology identifiable in 1972 will be in general use on college and university campuses."

Nine Technologies

In a 1972 MIT study by Jarrod W. Wilcox, "90 technologists who had participated in various national conferences on educational technology and 152 faculty members representing a broad, national cross section of views chose dates by which the nine basic technologies would be in 'routine use.'"

The nine technologies were defined by Wilcox as follows:

1. Routine audiovisual techniques—The classroom use of films, taped lectures shown on closed-circuit television or in listening laboratories, etc.

2. Programmed instruction. The student uses a text or simple supplementary device which employs step-by-step feedback reinforcement techniques to progress through sequentially ordered, structured material. Examples are programmed texts and self-study language audiotapes.

3. Routine computer-assisted instruction. The computer is used in the instructional process for either computerized programmed instruction or for drill and practice exercises.

4. Computer simulation. The computer is used in exercises involving student investigation of the properties of a "pseudo-reality" generated by a model of the phenomenon under study.

5. Advanced computer-assisted instruction. The computer is used in a flexible, individualized way to support student exploration of a well-defined body of knowledge; this may include Socratic dialog, tutorial exercises, and the ability to answer at least some unforeseen student questions.

6. Computer-managed instruction. Measures of the student's performance are monitored and analyzed by the computer; based on this the computer provides aid or direction to the student or teacher as to the most suitable packet of instructional material, such as film, programmed instruction, or live teacher, to be used next.

7. Remote classroom broadcasting and response. The use of remote television broadcasting from a central location to dispersed classrooms, with at least audio-live responses or questions from the students.

8. Student-initiated access to audiovisual recordings. The audiovisual recordings in a technological environment as sufficiently inexpen-

sive and easy to use to allow individual student-initiated access to recorded lectures or demonstration material.

9. Computer-aided course design. The use of computers to record and analyze student responses to instructional packets in computer-assisted and computer-managed instruction in order to provide information for the design of improvements in the instructional material

Technologists predicted that six of the nine technologies would be in routine use before 1980 and that all of them would be in routine use by 1990.

The technology prophets predicted what could have happened and probably should have happened, but didn't.

Take the Onus off the Faculty

More faculty might be willing, even eager to join the "technological revolution" if they were knowledgeable about the technology and skilled in its use. Doctoral programs and in-service programs for faculty already teaching should provide familiarization with technology.

The Carnegie Commission said:

> . . . faculty members of the future will need more training in the new instructional techniques. We believe that the Doctor of Arts degree we have recommended earlier is particularly adapted to the new situation. . . . [W]e recommended that the new Doctor of Arts degree offered by some institutions in the United States should be widely accepted as a degree for the "nonresearch teacher." It would require "(a) a broader field of basic knowledge than the more specialized Ph.D. degree, and (b) an opportunity to study and practice pedagogic technique."
>
> This recommendation becomes especially urgent if instructional technology is to be fully and wisely utilized. Institutions offering the proposed Doctor of Arts degree or other courses of instruction designed to prepare college and university teachers should provide instruction and experience in course development and the utilization of learning resources and instructional technologies as a part of their curricula.

The New Revolution

In the mid-1990s, some leading institutions were not only predicting a revolutionary technological future, but were planning how to bring it about. "This time, campus officials say, technology will transform academe as never before," says Robert L. Jacobson in the April 27, 1994, issue of the *Chronicle of Higher Education*, in which he surveys what was being discussed and planned on a number of campuses in response to burgeoning educational technological developments.

According to Jacobson, these campus officials say they need to "figure out which electronic, organizational, and instructional techniques can best help their institutions accommodate the increasing scope and pace of technological change."

Stanford University's President Gerhard Casper agreed that "the latest technology will transform both the content and delivery of higher education to an extent not yet fully understood or appreciated on most campuses."

Here's the real "fantastic fantasy future." Some college officials say a technology-driven restructuring of academe is only five to ten years away.

"In light of such analyses, leading-edge institutions have embarked on some of the most searching reassessments of technology's role in higher education since personal computers began sweeping across the country in the early 1980s."

The Doctor of Arts degree was pioneered at Carnegie-Mellon University. Interestingly enough, Carnegie-Mellon is in the forefront of those "leading-edge" institutions with top-notch technological instructional systems who are engaged in a serious study "to ponder what they have accomplished with technology so far, and what they might try to do next."

"John Bravman, chairman of a Stanford (University) subcommittee that is focusing on 'technique and technology in teaching and learning,' says that with options like two-way video conferencing, 'one can imagine rethinking the whole purpose and structure and function of a university like Stanford.'"

The University of Michigan is expecting a multi-million-dollar grant this spring to explore "how their courses may need to be revised to take advantage of new digital opportunities."

As in 1972, two problems will continue to inhibit the spread of technology: high costs and limited participation by many faculty members, says Jacobson in the *Chronicle of Higher Education*. There will be other problems also.

The Internet and the New Millennium

As the year 2000 unfolded, it began to reveal the awesome positive, the problematic, and the frightening negative potential of the Internet for worldwide communication.

The possible impact on higher education was addressed in a report issued in March of 2000 by Market Data Retrieval (MDR), a Dun and Bradstreet educational research company.

A number of colleges offer individual courses and even complete degree programs on the Internet.

And as colleges increased their use of the Internet to provide classes leading to degrees for students far away, on-campus students also reaped benefits that improved school life, the MDR report pointed out. The study showed that colleges also spent more money on technology, and added computers to dorms and classrooms.

Researchers surveying four thousand institutions found that seven out of ten colleges offered some form of distance learning, including courses, lecture notes, and online study groups. For 1999–2000, 34 percent of two- and four-year colleges offered degrees via computer, compared to 15 percent the previous year.

"The Internet is making life easier for students attending class and living on campus," said Mike Subrizi of MDR. But it is too soon, researchers and other educators say, to predict a nation of college students perched in front of dorm or home computers instead of in class.

"It would make no sense to bring people together in a physical setting and not have interpersonal interaction," said Stan Ikenberry, president of the American Council on Education. "That's the whole reason for having a campus in the first place."

But the rapid recent increased interest in distance learning continues. "As schools facing more competition from for-profit groups create their own online offerings, a college 'education' might one day be available for free."

Michael Saylor, chief executive of Microstrategy in Vienna, Virginia, told a group of Washington-based philanthropists on March 15, 2000, that he would donate $100 million to create a nonprofit, tuition-free online university that would offer an "Ivy League" education to anyone.

And six of the world's top educational institutions, including Columbia University and the London School of Economics and Political Science, are forming "the premier site for knowledge and education on the Internet."

The for-profit Internet site will have many free offerings, but other information will be provided for a fee. Advertising is also expected to be a component of the Web site.

Internet Pros and Cons

While students are and will continue to benefit from the Internet, it will create many problems for universities, such as how an institution can respond when other universities start offering electronic classes to its students.

But the frightening aspect of the Internet is the ease with which an increasing number of hackers have been able to exploit cyberspace's lack of legal protections and the extent of the damage hackers can do.

For example, in early May of 2000 a wake-up call was sent by the Love Bug virus, which emanated from a shabby, lower-middle-class neighborhood in Manila in the Philippines. It infected millions of computers around the world in Europe, North America, Asia, and Australia, causing massive damage. The crippling virus caused computers to crash and an estimated $12 billion in damages. The ease and the rapidity with which the virus multiplied stunned computer experts.

The exciting, positive possibilities as well as the great peril of the Internet for higher education must be thoroughly studied without delay.

What students need to learn and how they learn best must guide all considerations of the development of plans for the use of the Internet in the education process. The misguided concepts of many faculty (1) that college teaching's goal is to transmit considerable information from the mind of the professor to the mind of the student; and (2) that the lecture (although considered a very ineffective means by teaching-learning experts) is *the* method of college teaching are ill-founded.

Without considerable alteration or even the discarding of those concepts, no amount of technological innovation is likely to provide much, if any, of the improvement in undergraduate education envisioned by the Wingspread Group, the Boyer Commission, and other individual and group reformers.

TWELVE

THE ACADEMIC PROGRAM

There have been a number of prominent developments in curriculum evolution in American higher education, but a cursory look at curricula at Harvard, from its inception as the first college to modern times, gives a skeletal look at the extent of curricular change.

The Harvard curriculum of 1636, in which there was one course of study (sequence of courses) taken by all students, evolved into an elective system by 1886, in which an undergraduate could earn the A.B. degree by passing any eighteen courses, no two of which needed to be related.

In 1909 Harvard modified the elective system by adopting a plan with the purely elective principle giving way to a combination of required subjects and electives, which is characteristic of most college and university curriculums in the United States in the twenty-first century.

The emergence of the American university in the late nineteenth century—the result of the coming together of the English college tradition, the research ideal of the German university, and the American ideal of the university as an instrument of public service—bombarded the old curriculum with an expansion of new subjects, courses, programs, and degrees.

The American Association of Colleges study report in the mid-1980s states:

> As for what passes as a college curriculum, almost anything goes.
>
> The undergraduate major dominates, but the absence of a rationale for the major becomes evident when the college catalog says, pick eight of the following courses. And "the following" might be over a hundred courses, all served up as equals.

It is unlikely, whatever the major or institution, that the average graduating senior has any integrated sense of his or her major discipline and its links to other fields of inquiry.

The AAC report further says that undergraduate general education programs "lack a rationale and cohesion, or, even worse, are almost lacking altogether."

As a partial remedy for the conditions described, the AAC report suggests that the following nine experiences are essential to a good college education:

COHERENT UNDERGRADUATE EDUCATION

The AAC Plan

1. Inquiry, abstract logical thinking, critical analysis.
   To reason well, to recognize when reason and evidence are not enough, to discover the legitimacy of intuition, to subject inert data to the probing analysis of the mind—these are the primary experiences required of the undergraduate course study.
2. Literacy: writing, reading, speaking, listening.
3. Understanding numerical data requires a sophisticated level of understanding.
4. Historical consciousness. . . . A consciousness of history allows us to impose some intellectual order on the disorder of random facts. . . . History is all over the course of study.
5. Science . . . the world is less bewildering to someone who understands the nature of science, its methods, its reliability, and its limitations.
6. Values. [Men and women] must embody the values of a democratic society in order to fulfill the responsibilities of citizenship. They must be equipped to be perceptive and wise critics of society, repositories of the values that make civilized and humane society possible.
7. Arts. The languages of art, music, architecture, drama, and dance open up new worlds of human endeavor and communication, of truth and of representation. . . . Without a knowledge of the language of the fine arts, we see less and hear less.

8. International and multicultural experiences. To broaden the horizons of understanding for men and for women, therefore, colleges must provide them with access to the diversity of cultures and experiences that define American society and the contemporary world.

9. Study in depth. The minimum required curriculum that we here propose does not consist of required courses or prescribed subjects. Our concern is what happens to students when they study subjects and take courses in the various academic disciplines. Our focus is the methods and processes, the modes of access to understanding and judgment, that shape their undergraduate education.

   Depth requires sequential learning, building on blocks of knowledge that lead to more sophisticated understanding and encourage leaps of the imagination and efforts at a synthesis.

   Depth requires the kind of focused inquiry that takes time—for example, the year-long essay, the senior thesis, the artistic project, etc.

GENERAL EDUCATION

In his book *College: The Undergraduate Experience in America*, which summarizes the several-year Carnegie study in 1987, Boyer discusses concerns about the perceived overall weakness of the undergraduate curriculum, and the perception that revised and revitalized general education is urgently needed. Boyer asks the question:

> Can the American College, with its fragmentation and competing special interests, define shared academic goals? Is it possible to offer students, with their separate roots, a program of general education that helps them see connections and broadens perspective?
>
> We found during our study that general education is the neglected stepchild of the undergraduate experience. Colleges offer a smorgasbord of courses, and students pick and choose their way to graduation.
>
> Too many campuses, we found, are divided by narrow departmental interests that become obstacles to learning in the richer sense . . . protecting departmental turf often seemed more important than shaping a coherent general education program.

On the positive side for general education, Boyer says in *College*: "We found a longing among undergraduates for a more coherent view of knowledge. . . ." and ". . . the need to put their own lives in perspective." About general education courses where great teachers link learning to contemporary issues, Boyer says: "Almost without exception, classes such as these attract large crowds. . . ." Concerning faculty perceptions, Boyer states: "Faculty agree on the number of credits for a baccalaureate degree, but not on the meaning of a college education." Some figures he presents seem to reinforce that view:

> Today, 95 percent of all four-year colleges offer some form of general education. And since 1970, requirements in English, philosophy, Western civilization, third-world courses and international education have modestly increased. The greatest increases have been in computer literacy, mathematics, and the arts. However, during the same period, foreign language and physical education requirements were reduced. Even with these changes, it should be noted that only three subjects—English, math, and the arts—are required by 60 percent or more of the colleges.

In his book *College* Boyer also describes a visit to a university that had recently approved a new general education—or distribution—program: "The 'distribution' requirements now in place is typical at over 90 percent of the colleges and universities in the nation. All students at this college must now complete a course in English and mathematics, and at least one semester in foreign language. Beyond this, students select thirty units of credit from literally dozens of other courses spread among the humanities, natural sciences, and social sciences divisions."

What is needed, he concludes, is more coherence "to relate the core program to the lives of students and to the world they are inheriting."

He calls for the "integrated core . . . a program of general education that introduces students not only to essential knowledge, but also to connections across the disciplines, and, in the end, to the application of knowledge to life beyond the campus."

Boyer emphasizes: "General education is not a single set of courses. It is a program with a clear objective, one that can be achieved in a variety of ways. And while there may be great flexibility in the process, it is the clarity of purpose that is crucial."

As one approach to the development of an effective general education core, Boyer suggests the following cross-discipline, seven-areas-of-inquiry framework:

Boyer's Carnegie Plan

[1] Language: The Crucial Connection. . . . The sending and receiving of sophisticated messages set human beings apart from all other forms of life.

What are the theories of the origins of language? How do symbol systems shape the values of a culture? How has language, through great literature, enriched our lives and enlarged our vision? What are the possibilities and problems introduced by the information revolution?

[2] Art: The Esthetic Dimension. To express our most intimate, most profoundly moving feelings and ideas we use a more sensitive language we call the arts . . . music, dance, and the visual arts.

[3] Heritage: The Living Past. . . . [T]he study of history can strengthen awareness of tradition, of heritage, of meaning beyond the present.

The understanding of the past offers some hope for the improvement of the future.

[4] Institutions: The Social Web. [Acquaint students with] the major institutions—the family, the church, legislative and judicial bodies—that make up our world . . . what institutions have to do with us, how we are influenced by them, and how we can direct our institutions toward constructive ends.

[5] Nature: Ecology of the Planet. All the forms of life on the planet Earth are interlocked. No core of learning is complete without introducing students to the ordered yet symbiotic nature of the universe. For this discovery, science is the key.

[6] Work: The Value of Vocation. The characteristics of a culture can be defined by looking at work: who works; what work is valued; how it is rewarded; how do people use their leisure time? . . . [I]t is important for colleges to help students to consider the universal experiences of producing and consuming, and put their work in larger context.

[7] Identity: The Search for Meaning. Ultimately, the aim of common learning is the understanding of oneself and a capacity for sound judgment. . . . Sound judgment at its best brings purpose and meaning to human lives. Some of these [7] themes may call for special interdisciplinary or thematic courses. In other instances, existing departmental

courses in English, history, sociology, or science, if broad in their purpose, may effectively fit the bill.

The AAC report seeks a way to "a coherent undergraduate education," through an approach to the total curriculum. The Carnegie study report as presented by Boyer concentrates on helping students "see connections and broaden perspectives" through an integrated general education core program.

The AAC report discusses types of experiences, while Boyer discusses themes—areas of inquiry—as the means to a coherent undergraduate education. The reports emphasize that "what is being recommended is not a set of required subjects or academic disciplines," or "a single set of courses."

THE MORE STRUCTURED *50 HOURS* PLAN

A more specific model core curriculum was proposed in a report in 1989 by Dr. Lynne V. Cheney, then chairperson of the National Endowment for the Humanities.

Dr. Cheney said: "Strict core curricula taught by colleges' most distinguished professors would help cure the ills of undergraduate education."

The report, *50 Hours: A Core Curriculum for College Students*, was presented as colleges continued their efforts to make undergraduate education more coherent. Studies showed that some 95 percent of colleges were reworking their general-education programs. However, Dr. Cheney said that a Gallup survey and her research showed they were not tightening requirements enough.

According to the *50 Hours* report, "Colleges still allow students to fulfill general education requirements with a long list of narrowly focused courses rather than with broad-based studies that introduce classic texts and promote analytic thinking."

In *50 Hours*, Dr. Cheney criticizes college professors for "caring more about research than teaching. The stature of general education is diminished when a college or university's most distinguished faculty do not teach in it." Dr. Cheney continues:

At the center of "50 Hours" are six suggested survey courses on "cultures and civilizations" that include primary texts. History, literature, philosophy, and art are at the heart of this curriculum.

During their first semester, freshmen would consider "the origins of civilization" on several continents.

In their second and third semesters, students would tackle Western civilization from Periclean Athens through the twentieth century. Next . . . would be a core course in American civilization.

In their junior year, students would study other cultures.

50 Hours students should also take: "Two years of a foreign language. . . . A one-year course that explains 'the scope and power of mathematics, its beauty and challenge and the methods it brings to bear on problems.' . . . How computers help to pose and solve problems would also be taught. A one-year laboratory course that focuses on methods and ideas in the physical and biological sciences. . . . A one-year course that explores the 200-year influence of the social sciences."

A single institutional curriculum was long since made impractical by the development in America of diverse colleges and universities, and by the vast development of new knowledge. Similarly, a universal general education core cannot be prescribed for American institutions of higher education because of differences of institutional missions and goals and clientele.

But the AAC recommendations for types of experiences, Boyer's suggestions of areas of inquiry, and the more prescribed *50 Hours* plan can be very helpful to faculties and administrators as they seek to provide a framework for a cohesive and meaningful undergraduate curriculum.

THE PROCESS OF DEVELOPING THE UNDERGRADUATE CURRICULUM

The first step in developing such a curriculum for an individual college or university must be the clarifying of the goals of the institution—a clear and independent vision of what the institution's bachelor's degree recipient ought to know, ought to know how to do, and ought to be.

A sample of such goals, taken from the catalog of a small state university, follows:

1. skills of inquiry, abstract and logical thinking, and critical analysis;
2. literacy in writing, reading, listening, and speaking;
3. the ability to understand and use numbers and statistics;
4. a knowledge of world, national, and regional history;
5. an understanding of the scientific method;
6. an awareness of systems of values as bases for fulfilling the responsibilities of citizenship in a democratic society;
7. a sensitivity to the fine arts;
8. an awareness of the diverse cultures and experiences that define the contemporary world;
9. an understanding of human behavior and skills necessary for appropriate social interaction; and
10. a concentration in a discipline in order to enter a chosen profession, undertake advanced study, or develop an avocation.

Too often at colleges and universities, some such statement of goals for student achievement are placed in the institution's catalog, but there is no follow-up. There are no specific steps taken to help the students achieve the goals.

Once the goals are firmly and clearly established, a curriculum and a teaching strategy to implement the goals must be devised. Here, the overwhelming emphasis on specialization in graduate schools and undergraduate colleges becomes an almost insurmountable obstacle.

Graduate schools that provide doctoral programs for those who will become faculty members and administrators must provide (1) breadth that transcends courses and disciplines, (2) knowledge and experience that will enable the graduate students to someday visualize clear and comprehensive institutional goals, and (3) curricula and teaching strategies for interdisciplinary coherence.

Since few graduate schools have been providing the above three educational experiences, undergraduate colleges will need to provide them in in-service programs.

The preparation of undergraduate college faculty, in doctoral programs and/or in in-service programs, to be effective participants in integrated, coherent undergraduate education will likely need reinforcement.

The *blueprint plan* mentioned earlier can be an effective means of reinforcement. Under the plan, each faculty member would develop a blueprint for each course he or she was to teach, including goals for the course, specific means planned to achieve the goals, means for assessment of student achievement, a tentative course outline, a time-table, and a bibliography.

Before the beginning of a term or year, the department chairperson would meet with each department member to discuss how, in each course, he or she planned to weave total institutional goals into the course where feasible, and achieve coherence between course materials and other areas of knowledge.

For instance, looking at the example of a state university's goals provided earlier, goal 2—literacy in writing, reading, listening, and speaking—could be included, along with the specific subject matter of the course, in most course plans, as could goal 1—skills of inquiry, abstract and logical thinking, and critical analysis—and some of the other goals.

In regard to some of the goals such as number 6—an awareness of systems of values as bases for fulfilling the responsibilities of citizenship in a democratic society—a course in the core may be required, but some emphasis on values can likely be provided in most courses, and in actions by the institution.

Faculty members should be made aware that they have a responsibility to further the implementation of the institution's goals, where feasible, in their courses and elsewhere.

Obstacle # 19
Adherence to Credit Hour System

The AAC, Carnegie, and *50 Hours* reports represent different levels of flexibility in recommendations for providing more coherence and comprehensiveness to undergraduate education. Each of the three recommended programs offers possibilities that would improve the undergraduate programs of a great many colleges and universities.

The AAC talks about nine experiences essential to a good undergraduate education, those experiences to be translated into courses.

Boyer calls for a "seven areas of inquiry framework" for an integrated core providing essential knowledge, connections across disciplines, and application of knowledge to life beyond the campus—all to be provided primarily through courses.

Cheney's Humanities program would encompass a core of fifty hours with specific course areas to be explored in specific semesters in specific years.

All rely on the near-universal practice of measuring a student's education by counting credit hours—the number of hours a student spends in classes.

Is such a method the best way to determine outcomes, that is, how well a student has achieved the basic goals of an undergraduate education? Ah, there's the rub. What are the goals of an undergraduate education? Many answers have been given, among them the following:

- Students need to develop skills of analysis, synthesis, and reasoning.
- Students need to understand the interrelatedness of knowledge—see it as a connected web instead of many isolated segments and bits.
- Key elements of an undergraduate education are communication, critical thinking, and quantitative reasoning.

Could not such goal achievement be better judged and encouraged through assessment of academic competence of students demonstrated on broad-based examinations? As Clara Lovett suggested in the November 2, 1995, *Chronicle of Higher Education*: "Institutions wishing to move toward competence-based exams could draw on the experience of the assessment movement, now more than 10 years old."

It would also be helpful to examine information about the Alverno College experiment, briefly discussed in chapter 10 among the excerpts from my monograph: "Preserving the Private College—and Diversity."

Radical Recommendation 55
Emphasis on Outcomes

Place less emphasis on the accumulation of student credit hours and time in the classrooms, and move to assessment through competency-based, broad examinations.

Obstacle #20
Program Reform

The doctoral preparation of faculty and their teaching areas are so narrow that it will be very difficult for them to contribute to establishing overall goals for undergraduate education and core curriculums.

Radical Recommendation 56
Faculty Preparation

Doctoral preparation must be more broad and provide guidance into integrated curriculum and course development; and in-service preparation of faculty for development of institutional goals and a general education core should center on reports such as the AAC, Carnegie, *50 Hours*, and others.

Obstacle #21
Vast Program Reform

The entrenchment of incrementalism as the means of bringing about change in the overwhelming majority of colleges and universities will make the sweeping program changes called for in the Wingspread report and the Boyer Commission report extremely difficult to achieve.

Radical Recommendation 57
Program Reform

With firm backing by the governing board, the president should provide strong leadership to faculty, academic administrators, and board members in a review and reconstruction of the institution's goals for students.

It is most important that an institution's purpose and goals for the twenty-first century are clearly defined. The overall guiding question must be, what do our students need? What should our graduates be, know, and know how to do?

Once updated purpose and goals are established, planning for implementation is the next step. General education requirements consisting of a smorgasbord of a large number of narrow, specialized courses will lead to the continuation of a fragmented undergraduate education lamented by AAC, Carnegie, *50 Hours*, and other reports.

Paula Brownlee, AAC president says: "All students need help to link knowledge across discipline boundaries, and numbers of institutions are developing general education 'core curricula' to replace distribution courses."

There appears to be a growing faculty interest in the core concept, although not yet widespread. In 1991 Carl A. Raschke was the founding president of the American Association for the Advancement of Core Curriculum, the goal of which was to promote the development of more coherent general education programs for undergraduates.

For an example of a core course, let us look at the sciences. In an article in the *Chronicle of Higher Education*, Professors Robert M. Hazen and James Trefil state that "the average college graduate is scientifically illiterate . . . [a person] who can't understand the simplest science-related newspaper article." This is the result of institutions offering only introductory courses focusing on specific disciplines.

Hazen and Trefil continue: "Science forms a web of knowledge about the universe, and the key to scientific literacy is general science education. To produce scientifically literate graduates, colleges must offer courses that encompass all the physical and life sciences, emphasizing general principles rather than esoteric detail."

Other interdisciplinary courses or problem-centered courses might be used in a core.

A course on values would answer the strong concern expressed in the Wingspread report, but a concern about values should be found in courses across the campus, and in the performance of the university, for example, in its athletic program.

A course about religions, advocating no particular religion, would help students gain personal understanding and understandings about world religion problems.

A course about drugs (especially alcohol, which is a major campus problem, and will be a lifetime problem for many students) should be given strong consideration.

Radical Recommendations 58–59
Goal Implementation

58. A general education core should be established to play a major role in implementing the newly developed purpose and goals.

59. Institutional goals should not only be pursued in general education core courses, but also in all courses.

Most colleges and universities have lofty goals expressed in their catalogs and promotional materials, but how many implement their goals in their academic programs? Likely, few have assessment programs to compare outcomes with institutional goals.

It is suspected that too often a faculty member is hired because of an academic specialty, assigned to a department, and turned loose to do his thing within the specialty, likely with little or no administrative attention to what he teaches or how he teaches.

Obstacle #22
Effective Instruction

It seems that many administrators and faculty members have a mistaken idea of what academic freedom is and is not. For our purposes here, we will simply point out what it is not.

It is not license for the faculty member to define his role and perform it as he wishes. It does not give the faculty member the right to do a poor job of teaching, and it does not give the faculty member the right to pursue only his goals in his classes while ignoring institutional goals.

The institution should not leave to chance the quality of a faculty member's teaching, nor her incorporation of institutional goals into her courses and advising.

How can the institution achieve the above without violating the faculty member's academic freedom?

Radical Recommendation 60
Sensible Supervision

An institution should use a modified management by objectives system, and course blueprints to affect the quality of teaching and the pursuit of the institutional goals by faculty.

First, institutional goals for student achievement are established by faculty, administration, and governing board.

Next, in individual meetings with each staff member who reports directly to him or her, the president clearly enunciates the institutional goals. Each staff member is asked to formulate a job plan for himself for the year, incorporating the institutional goals, where feasible, into the plan, the means to achieve the goals, and methods of assessment of achievement of the goals. At the end of the year, each staff member will be evaluated on his success in achieving the goals that he helped establish.

This process will be followed from the vice presidents to the deans or other unit heads, from the deans and other subunit heads to department chairpersons, and from department heads to faculty and others reporting to persons at the chairperson level.

In the case of faculty, the department chairperson, or assistant chairperson in a very large department, should discuss the institution's goals for students with each faculty member individually. Then each faculty member should be asked to develop a blueprint for each course she will teach during the year. Each course blueprint should include the instructor's discipline goals and institutional goals that are feasible in the particular course, specific means for achieving each goal, and specific means for assessment of student achievement in regard to each goal. The instructor should be the determinant of the final blueprint plan, and she should be evaluated on the success of the students in achieving the course goals in the blueprint.

MBO should be used similarly in nonacademic units to further the carrying out of institutional goals campus wide.

Obstacle #23
Primary Program Determinant

There is an increasingly heard perception, right or wrong, that institutional welfare and faculty desires often supersede student needs in the development and implementation of the academic program.

Radical Recommendation 61
Student Needs

Not just the general education core, but the entire education program should be based on what students need.

College and university catalogs list many frivolous courses such as the "The Seduced Maiden Motif in German Literature" and "Sources of the Music in Shakespeare's Comedies." Likely, very few undergraduates have a need for such courses, but they were courses a faculty member wanted to teach. No doubt many courses arise out of a faculty member's special interest, even a dissertation, without regard to their value to students.

Such courses use faculty members' time that could be better spent, for example, in the development and teaching of something students need—a beginning general course in each department which would present the basic principles of the discipline, interrelated with concepts of other disciplines, and related to life.

Student Retention

According to the alarming drop-out rates—four-year institutions graduate only an average of about 50 percent of the students who matriculate on their campuses—there is a great need for more student retention programs.

Studies indicate that many drop out because they are not well served by their college or university. Top retention expert Dr. Lee Noel says that at most institutions without good retention programs, the development of such programs can reduce the drop-out rate by one-third.

Research shows that the first six weeks of the freshman year are crucial for potential drop-outs. That's why "front-loading" programs have had great success. In such a program, presemester orientation is provided, and possibly even an orientation course; students are tested in regard to their readiness for a particular course; thorough initial and continuing academic advising is provided; and the best and most caring professors teach the beginning courses.

The University of Iowa has had success with a scheduling plan in which freshman volunteers are assigned to groups, which are then registered as groups for core general education classes. The same students in several classes together get to know each other, are supportive of each other, sometimes study together, and get a sense of belonging in the small group on a large campus. The effect on the students has been very positive.

PROGRAM INEFFICIENCIES

Academic programs on a great many college and university campuses are replete with inefficiencies. There may be courses, especially in a major field, that overlap, that deal with much the same material in two, three, even eight or nine courses.

For example, in a journalism department there may be nine or more courses dealing with writing in each—courses such as Reporting, Reporting of Public Affairs, Newswriting I, Newswriting II, Radio Newswriting, TV Newswriting, Feature Writing, Editorial Writing, and Magazine Article Writing. Eliminating duplication might leave three of four courses such as Reporting, Newswriting, Journalistic Writing Forms I, and Journalistic Writing Forms II.

The size of the journalism staff could be reduced, and students would have time to take other broadening courses.

This is not meant to single out journalism programs for criticism. Similar scrutiny of other departments' programs would likely often find comparable unnecessary duplication.

Another example of inefficiency might be the allowing of a statistics course in each of a number of departments, with each course concentrating on the subject matter of the department. This could well result in small statistics classes in some departments, and each department would have to have a statistics expert on its staff.

The alternative would be to have statistics taught in one department—mathematics—with application being made to various disciplines. Feasible class sizes could be maintained, and fewer statistics experts would be needed.

Classes that continually attract very small enrollments and are not essential to the program should be dropped or offered less frequently.

Required courses that frequently attract very small enrollments should be offered less frequently, for example every other year in a regular pattern. Well-informed, alert advisers would have the responsibility of preventing a situation in which a senior would need a course that would not be offered until the following year.

Offering majors in a number of foreign languages can be costly because enrollments, especially in advanced courses, can be small. Several neighboring institutions can deal with this problem by each offering majors in different languages, and arranging for their students to be able to study a language in another institution. Or, two institutions located as much as one hundred miles apart might make joint appointments of one or more language instructors who would spend two days a week on each campus.

Ongoing Curricular Development: Strategic Planning

A college or a university is not a static institution in a static society. The development of new knowledge and new needs dictate that an institution that is to serve well must operate with some degree of flexibility and stability. Colleges and universities cannot be blown hither and yon by every changing breeze—get caught up in every fad. It is important, therefore, that the institutions develop an approach that will provide responsible flexibility. One such approach would be through strategic planning.

Strategic planning is planning for the future. It is not the preparation of a voluminous plan developed in a concentrated, short-term effort. It is a continuous process. It is not the work of a professional planner. It seeks involvement of the entire campus and related constituencies.

Planning implies change. Two things are essential prerequisites for change. First, the mission and goals of the institution must be clearly delineated and articulated. Second, the institution must be as effective as it can be before it launches into change.

On the latter point, it must be remembered that a major portion of the operations on most campuses is nonacademic—housing, dining halls and cafeterias, security forces, buses and other vehicles, travel, counseling and medical services, placement offices, campus maintenance, athletics, bookstores—all lend themselves to the finest business practices, as to some extent do the academic activities.

The quality of employees is most important. Weak links must be strengthened and the quality of new employees—faculty, administration, and other—must be carefully monitored.

Adequate facilities and equipment in good condition are other important considerations.

While the establishment of a clear mission and long-range goals are very important, it must be reiterated that strategic planning is not the development of a detailed plan for the future of the institution.

Strategic planning is a continual process of information gathering, analysis, and decision making. It is action-oriented, looking to implementation. If the institution is not functioning efficiently and if it does not have quality staff operating in good facilities with adequate equipment, launching into change might not only place the change in jeopardy, but also endanger the stability of the entire institution.

In *Academic Strategy*, George Keller says that the fundamental aim of strategic planning is linking the forward direction of the institution with the movement of historical forces in the environment. Two critical areas for analysis are one's own organization and the environment.

A college needs to examine the internal traditions and values, and strength and weaknesses of its programs, faculty, location, size, finances, etc.

Then, Keller explains, an institution needs to take a careful look at the external world.

> What are the likely developments in electronics, high school populations, energy costs, federal policy, and the national and regional economy? How will they affect you? What new opportunities might they open up? What are likely to be the frontiers of academic research and study? Who are your competitors and how are they responding to these frontiers and to their threats and opportunities? And what segments of the higher education market do you now serve? How do the various seg-

ments of the market perceive your institution, and its strengths and weaknesses? What are the growing and declining demand areas for your programs?

Your academic strategy . . . should exude from this compound of internal and external considerations.

Dr. John Millet, former university president and system chancellor, prominent consultant, and expert and prolific writer on organization, administration, and effective operation of colleges and universities, states unequivocally: "The planning effectiveness of a campus depends on the planning effectiveness of its presidential leadership. . . . The initiative for planning must come from the president." These words appeared in George Keller's 1983 book titled *Academic Strategy.*

A cabinet or council of administration and faculty leaders may serve as interactors in strategic planning, but the president should thoroughly and clearly explain strategic planning to faculty and administrators, and ask for the active engagement of the minds of all in the ongoing process.

Such a thorough process should enable a college or university to develop and maintain a curriculum that would meet the current and changing needs of students and society, and strengthen the viability of the institution.

Potential Problem Sources

As any college prepares to revise its overall curriculum and/or its general education program, it should be aware of some sources of potential problems.

Dr. Donald Kagan, dean of Yale College, was quoted in a June 1991 issue of the *Chronicle of Higher Education* as follows: "Dr. Kagan lamented the lack of a common curriculum at Yale, but said he had no intention of trying to introduce one. Not only would the faculty not approve it, it would be far more terrible if the faculty did approve it. Consider what a core constructed by the current faculty would look like, and the consequences that would ensue if they also had the responsibility of teaching it." He added that most were too narrowly educated to do so.

In another issue of the *Chronicle of Higher Education* in the late 1980s, Dr. Hunter R. Rawlings III of the University of Colorado is reported to have said: "The purpose of a liberal education has always been to enable students *to see things whole*. Today, however, the academic department structure makes that goal almost impossible to achieve at most colleges and universities by compartmentalizing knowledge mercilessly. . . . Today the business of departments is to train specialists, not to educate human beings."

In a June 1992 article in the *Chronicle of Higher Education*, Bryan Barnett of Rutgers University discusses how narrow preparation in doctoral programs and intensive work in a very narrow specialty by faculty adversely affects undergraduate curriculum.

Barnett says that the tremendous proliferation of college courses includes a vast number that represent professors' highly specialized interests rather than student needs. Such courses would be eliminated if curricula were developed with the needs of students in mind, based on the teaching faculty's formulation of a clear and independent vision of what the well-educated bachelor's degree recipient ought to know, ought to know how to do, and ought to be.

Of course, new courses will need to be developed and/or old courses revised when essential new knowledge is developed.

In many subject areas there is considerable duplication from course to course. Elimination of unnecessary course duplication could likely be achieved across campuses.

Specific Positive Considerations

The following are specific positive factors, (some of which were mentioned before, but are presented here for emphasis and depth of discussion) which should be considered by a college embarking on a total college or a general education curriculum revision.

In *The Search for a Common Learning*, Dr. Russell Thomas says: "The idea should be permanently dispelled that general education, because it aims at breadth of knowledge, must necessarily be shallow or superficial. Breadth of learning, properly ordered, is productive of its own kind of depth, of insights which no limited form of concentration can achieve."

Thomas also says that there ought to be, in every considered field, a general course (for nonmajors) designed to give a comprehension of its underlying principles.

General education should not be something that students "get out of the way" as soon as possible so that they can get into their major. In the first college semesters, it can help a student who is undecided about a major to gain perspective.

General education should span three or four years. The students can better integrate knowledge and gain an overview perspective in the senior year after having studied a number of areas.

As campuses have achieved mega-size, some enrolling upwards of forty thousand students, an encompassing learning environment has disappeared from much of American higher education, and the goal of educating the whole student seems to have been abandoned, except in some small colleges.

While there can be no return to the early colleges where a tutor and a group of students shared living quarters, meals, academic experiences, and other college activities together for four years, educational coherence and student development could be significantly enhanced if faculty and administrators sought to provide something of a small college aura.

The Claremont Cluster

It may be physically impossible to divide universities into a number of small colleges as at Cambridge and Oxford, campuses that were initially designed for such division. However, in the Claremont University Center in California, five small colleges and a graduate school operate in a somewhat loose cluster system. They share a bookstore, library, campus security, health services, physical plant operation and maintenance, and purchasing. Each has its own academic specialties and its own general education program, although students may take individual courses in a college other than their own. Each college has a president, who meets with the other presidents in a Presidents' Council about common concerns. The colleges share in the financial benefit of the large, joint operation, while providing the educational and social atmosphere of the small college.

The Iowa Plan

Earlier, we briefly introduced the Iowa Plan (see page 160). In an issue of the *Chronicle of Higher Education*, Dr. Donald N. McCloskey discusses an attempt to provide more cohesion in undergraduate education for students in large universities by forming groups of students who will attend some general education classes together for the first couple of years. This can provide the unifying of social and intellectual life that students automatically get in small colleges, McCloskey says:

> Students can create a social life for themselves faster in a small group than they can as strangers in a class of 400. They soon go to classes as friends. Further, they begin to do intellectual work in common; they study together, they end up thinking about what they've learned together.
>
> Students in the program are lively, interactive, honest. They watch out for each other. Attendance is better than in similar classes of strangers, faculty members report, and discussions are easier to sustain.

McCloskey also suggests that the housing office could assign people in the same academic group to the same dormitory, creating numerous small colleges out of one big one, and at no extra cost.

The Iowa plan seems to have great potential for educational coherence and total student development. But the success of the plan would not only rest on the assignment of groups of students into classes and dorms together, but also on the development of a limited and specific group of general education core courses, rather than the smorgasbord of courses now offered by so many institutions.

At Michigan State

At Michigan State University in the early 1960s, a plan was developed to provide coherence and support for freshman students. In one building were dormitory rooms, a dining hall, classrooms, and offices of faculty who taught freshman courses. When not in class, the faculty were in their offices available to provide assistance to students, and trained counselors lived in the building to help students after the end of the faculty workday. Again, this plan would require at least a partial general education common core whose teachers could be housed in the building. A large, cafeteria-style offering of education courses would likely make it virtually impossible to provide office space for all the courses in the building.

The Iowa State and Michigan State plans provide some special conditions for beginning students that are conducive to improved student learning early on. This is in harmony with recommendations of experts on student retention.

STUDENT RETENTION

Student retention (see also page 159) is something that relatively few institutions do well, although the number is increasing. But it is a grave problem, and most colleges and universities need to give serious attention to it.

Dr. Lee Noel, one of the top researchers and experts in the field, points out that numerous institutions, public and private, graduate fewer than 50 percent of the freshmen who enter their institutions, and an even larger number of institutions graduate no more than one-third of their entering freshmen.

This represents institutional failure as much, if not more, as it does student failure.

There is considerable research on retention and there are proven solutions to the problem.

Thirty-two percent of entering freshmen drop out before the sophomore year. So the first year, especially the first six weeks, are extremely critical. Thus, the Iowa State and the Michigan State programs are on target by giving students extra support early. An early-attention program is termed "front-loading."

Notre Dame has established a freshman studies program with a dean and a staff. The attrition rate for the first year at Notre Dame was 1 percent instead of the national average of 32 percent in 1983, and the attrition rate through the senior year was between 6 and 7 percent instead of the 50 to 70 percent at so many institutions. There are a number of other retention success stories.

While faculty and administration need to attack the retention problem, a strong commitment from the president is essential because it is a campus-wide problem that requires participation from across the campus.

Once a president has made a strong commitment to a retention program, and a program director has been appointed and a structure established, a number of basic program components can be identified.

(a) It is very important that all employees—faculty, administration, clerical staff—be thoroughly informed about the program, its goals, and what they can do to help.

(b) A thorough student orientation should be planned, preferably for the summer preceding first enrollment. An orientation course in the first term has been found to be very helpful.

(c) A strong program of advising, beginning before the first term and continuing, is essential.

(d) Diagnostic testing of students in several areas is important, in order that the information can be used to get students into courses for which they are adequately prepared.

(e) Developmental courses should be established as needed. While some faculty may resist remediation, if an institution admits some students with some academic deficiencies, it is ethically bound to give them a fair chance to succeed.

(f) The first sessions taught in freshman courses are the most important of a student's college days. Instructors should make every effort to be helpful to the fledgling students.

(g) The best teachers in the institution, whether they are young instructors or experienced full professors, should teach freshman courses, especially during the first term. The teaching approach should be student centered in an encouraging class atmosphere by caring teachers.

(h) A coherent, interrelated curriculum should be provided. At Notre Dame, all freshmen take the same course format, including required general education courses and two electives each term.

(i) Involve students in the life of the campus, but caution students not to get overinvolved in nonacademic activities, especially in the first term.

Involving students with other students in academics, as in the Iowa scheduling plan, can also help give students a sense of belonging.

Students learn from their peers, so plan for this.

(j) Provide trained counselors in the dormitories.

A retention program is simply a means by which a college or a university musters all of its resources to focus on facilitating the success of its students. How can any institution justify doing any less?

CORE COURSE CONSIDERATIONS

An indication of an increasing recognition of the needs to improve college teaching and learning, and the curriculum is seen in the development of a clearinghouse for teaching, learning, and curricular innovations for colleges.

A consortium of interested colleges operates through a state-financed clearinghouse based at Evergreen State College. Called the Washington Center for Improving the Quality in Undergraduate Education, the clearinghouse has coordinated the development of course designs used by thirty-seven public and private colleges and universities. Those institutions have experimented with programs that emphasize collaborative teaching, thematically grouped courses, and writing across the curriculum. The center has also coordinated the development of several models for curricular change.

Every college or university should, of course, develop its own academic program to carry out its own mission and goals, but much can be learned from other institutions, as those participating in the Washington state consortium have discovered.

As we have seen, most experts call for a tighter core of general education graduation requirements in contrast to the fragmented, long lists of courses from which students select to meet graduation requirements at many institutions.

In designing or augmenting such a core, each individual institution might wish to examine, from its own perspective, the following:

Great Themes

Courses might be built around the expected great ideas or great issues of the twenty-first century. In his 1994 book, *Higher Education Cannot Escape History*, Clark Kerr listed the following as possible themes for individual courses:

- The roles of religion and nationality in modern life
- Issues of war and peace, and the general subject of conflict resolution

- The pathologies of industrial civilization
- Competition in the global economy

Many years ago in a private college with an enrollment of less than one thousand students, a faculty committee was formed to develop an honors program. They read all they could find on such programs; then they wrote to institutions that had honors programs, seeking to learn from others in the spirit of the Washington consortium.

The committee developed an honors program, a prominent part of which was an interdisciplinary theme or topic course. The first time the course was offered, the topic was "The Dehumanization of Man." Skilled teachers in a number of disciplines were invited by the course coordinator to participate in the course with fifteen honors students.

The class met for three hours once a week at night, with a faculty member from a different discipline presiding at each session. Each faculty member provided the students with a relevant reading list from his discipline one week before he was to preside.

The faculty member generally approached the course topic from the viewpoint of her discipline during the first part of the class, and the latter part of the class was devoted to discussion—often lively debate—based on the first part of the class and the readings the students had perused. As the course progressed beyond the first several meetings, an increasing number of references were made to points that had surfaced during prior class meetings that featured other disciplines. Some faculty members who had participated earlier came to later sessions that featured other disciplines.

Honors students often stayed up late into the night after class meetings, still debating; and a few faculty members teaching traditional classes complained that the few honors students in their classes were consumed by their interest in the honors course and neglected their work in the traditional classes.

The course generated great enthusiasm, and the honors students and participating faculty precipitated a ripple effect into other courses and throughout the campus.

Topical courses taught by stimulating teachers with an interdisciplinary approach have proved to be very popular in recent years. They encourage integrative thinking, which should be a very important part of a student's education.

In *Higher Education Cannot Escape History*, Kerr explains: "Students need to be actively involved in considering issues that cut across disciplinary boundaries, in order to attain a larger view of problems and their alternative solutions. Issues in the real world seldom fall neatly into the categories that we assign as school subjects, but instead involve aspects of a variety of subjects and require integrating ideas and methods from a variety of disciplines."

Values and Ethics

Of the Wingspread Group's thirty-two expert essayists responding to the question "What does society need from higher education?" twenty-two wrote about the need for higher education to engage more intensively with the issue of values.

Ethics are taught in specialized colleges such as business and medicine. But a course in values/ethics should be considered and a values/ethics emphasis could be incorporated into virtually every course in the institution.

Religion

The stunning and devastatingly successful Muslim terrorist attacks on New York and Washington were followed by terrorist leaders' threats that what we experienced was only the beginning of much more severe, widespread, and continuing attacks in the coming months and years.

Osama bin Laden and other terrorist leaders have been trying to whip up a religious frenzy among the one billion Muslims against the United States, with some initial success. It is at this point that American universities can play a significant role.

Americans generally have little knowledge or understanding of the Islamic religion or the Arab world, and the Muslims outside the United States have even less knowledge and understanding of American society.

A required course about the world's major religions should be provided in American universities. The course should not promote any specific religion, but rather concentrate on providing information and understanding about the various religions, emphasizing similarities rather than differences.

Faculty in other areas, such as political science, history, sociology, economics, and literature should be encouraged to incorporate information about the Muslim-Arab world into their classes where relevant and feasible.

The above two curricular recommendations will not be a quick fix, but over the years might provide an infusion of enlightenment about a critical part of the world to Americans.

Penetrating the closed Arab societies with similar enlightenment about America will be much more difficult.

The U.S. government must work much harder and smarter to get accurate information about America to the Arab people to counteract the distorted and hateful information transmitted to them by their governments and their mass media. Also, the 6 million Muslims living in the United States provide a unique opportunity for the development of a person-to-person "public relations" program. If a great many American Muslims were to inform their relatives and friends in Arab countries about the wonders of American society—its freedoms and its caring nature—this could be very useful in helping to establish amicable Arab-U.S. relations.

Of even greater long-term potential would be the vast increase of public and private scholarship money to bring Arab students to study at American universities. Currently only 5 percent of foreign students studying in America are from Arab countries. Bringing promising, young, prospective future Arab leaders to study in our universities will enable them to learn about the United States firsthand, and return to their countries and tell what they learned. A steady stream over the years of (hopefully) such positive "ambassadors" might do much to soften the U.S. image in Arab countries.

Science

The Wingspread Group concurs with Hazen and Trefil that "the average college graduate is scientifically illiterate." In their article in the *Chronicle of Higher Education*, Hazen and Trefil suggest the following remedy: "Science forms a web of knowledge about the universe, and the key to scientific literacy is general science education. To produce scientifically literate graduates, colleges must offer courses that encompass all the physical and life sciences, and emphasizing general principles rather than esoteric detail."

It is inconceivable that every core would not have at least one such general science course.

Similar other cross-discipline courses, emphasizing basic principles, should also be considered. Look to the AAC, Carnegie, and *50 Hour* proposals as well as other respected sources for ideas.

Internationalization

In *Troubled Times for American Higher Education* (1994), Kerr says that internationalization will be a great theme for the United States in the 1990s, when higher education will pay more attention to world history and to comparative cultures around the globe.

Surely there must be a strong international emphasis in one or more core courses, and an international perspective in a great many other courses.

The Foreign Language Question

Over the years during discussions about possible inclusions in general education requirements, foreign language has often been a major point of disagreement. A dean whose faculty was involved in a heated conflict about the possible inclusion of foreign language in the core, did a mail survey of more than one hundred foreign language department chairpersons. He asked: Should all college students be required to study a foreign language? If so, how much should be required? What benefits would students receive from the study of a foreign language?

The response to the dean's survey was excellent.

All who responded, predictably, said foreign language should be a graduation requirement, and two years of study was the minimum recommended. To the questions of why it should be required, and what benefits students would receive, numerous answers were given.

Again, predictably, the primary response was to gain "competence in the use of a foreign language, which all students need." A second was to gain an understanding of the people in a foreign country and their culture. A third was to get a better understanding of, and appreciation for language.

Of the many languages in the world, which one would be useful for a student?

How much competence in the use of a language can students expect to achieve in two years of study? Could real competence in use be better achieved in a semester or even less of concentrated language study, with students living in a dormitory where only the language being studied was spoken?

Could an understanding of a people and their culture not be achieved better in a one-semester course without the need to spend a major amount of time mastering vocabulary, grammar, sentence structure, idioms, etc. of a foreign language?

And, couldn't students get a better understanding of a language in a unit in an English course on the origin and development of language?

These are the kinds of questions that are often asked, and should be, just as penetrating questions should be asked about any other course being considered for inclusion in the required core. There should be a clear understanding about the specific reasons for the inclusion of every course in the general education core.

THIRTEEN

CONDUCT

CAMPUS CLIMATE AND VALUES

In "Universities in the Digital Age" in the July/August 1996 *Change* magazine, John Brown and Paul Duguid remind us that, "The knowledge delivery view . . . misunderstands how people learn, where they learn and when they learn. . . . [I]t portrays students as vessels into which the university pours information." As Brown and Duguid note, this view "takes no account of the active participation necessary for learning and knowing [and it] overlooks all the things that people learn on campus outside as well as inside the classroom."

This "outside" learning can be at least as important to the student as teacher-delivered knowledge. Learning outside the classroom has been given minimal attention in this volume thus far, but the estimated considerable volume of such learning does warrant a closer examination.

This chapter will cursorily examine the important campus learning environment from the standpoint of:

- how it is affected by student conduct;
- how it can be affected positively by the university's conduct;
- and how lifetime students' conduct can and should be affected by positive alteration of the campus environment, and by curricular and off-campus exploration of values, ethics, and morals.

175

Obstacle #24
The Campus Environment

In previous chapters, universities were severely criticized because of the flawed and inadequate classroom learning opportunities they offered to their undergraduates. Here, the cavalier neglect of the campus environment by many universities will also receive harsh criticism. Some critics have charged that many university campuses are anti-intellectual, raucous, out of control, dangerous, seemingly devoid of values, and hedonistic, constituting a campus climate in which a great many freshmen and many upperclassmen find it extremely difficult, if not impossible, to engage in serious and sustained intellectual activity.

While the critics' charges may be overstated, there is evidence that negative components on many campuses are serious impediments to the creation and maintaining of a learning-supportive campus environment.

Alcohol Abuse

Alcohol is the number one drug problem in this country. It shouldn't be surprising, then, that college presidents rank alcohol abuse as the number one problem on campus. Princeton University President Harold Shapiro has declared alcohol abuse the single greatest threat to the university's fulfillment of its mission.

In 1994, a commission convened by the Center on Addiction and Substance Abuse at Columbia University issued an alarmist report that indicated that one in three college students drinks to get drunk, and that the number of women drinking to get drunk more than tripled between 1977 and 1993, to a rate now equal to that of men.

A more recent college alcohol study by the Harvard School of Public Health gives an in-depth view of alcohol abuse in a cross section of American higher education. Nearly eighteen thousand students in forty states and from 140 colleges—two-thirds public, one-third private—filled out twenty-page surveys that asked them a variety of questions about their drinking behavior and explored problems they experienced as a result of their own and other students' drinking.

Binge drinking in the study was described as five or more drinks in a row, one or more times in a two-week period for men; for women, four or more drinks in a row.

Some findings of the study include the following:

Many students reported drinking far more for the purpose of getting drunk. Eighty-four percent drank during the school year. Forty-four percent were binge drinkers.

Bingeing rates varied dramatically from campus to campus, the lowest being 1 percent of the students, the highest 70 percent. At nearly one-third of the schools, more than half of the responding students were binge drinkers. Fraternities and sororities led in binge drinking: women in sorority houses, 80 percent; men in fraternity houses, 86 percent.

On campuses where more than half the students are binge drinkers, 87 percent of students living on campus have experienced one or more problems as a result of others' binge drinking. At high binge colleges, 26 percent of women reported an unwanted sexual advance in connection with others' alcohol use.

Henry Wechsler, a lecturer in the Harvard School of Public Health, in the July/August 1996 *Change* magazine says colleges with binge drinkers must ask: "Can we accomplish our mission and fulfill our students' goals if we tolerate behavior that compromises the quality of students' education and social lives, as well as their health and safety?"

And the problems are escalating. An Associated Press story in late May of 1998 began:

> Bonfires in the streets. Bottles whizzing by at police. Chants and tear gas and television footage of students led away in handcuffs.
>
> The images may have harkened back to the '60s, but it wasn't war or segregation that inspired scores of college students to take to the streets this year.
>
> **It was the right to party!**
>
> Students from at least 10 schools rallied and rioted, saying new restrictions on how they drink and carouse were the latest evidence that their freedom is at stake.

At Michigan State University, a student summoned three thousand fellow students through e-mail into the streets after the university banned drinking at a popular spot where students party before and after football games. Police fired teargas as students lit bonfires and threw rocks and bottles at police.

This must be looked on as a sad commentary on 1998 student activism.

Other Drug Problems

Dr. Robert LaLance, Vice President for Student Affairs at Middle Tennessee State University, and I have had many conversations about the concerns administrators have about drug use among college students. LaLance reports that he and his staff as well as some of his counterparts at other universities are being told by incoming freshmen that drug use in high school and in lower grades is increasing rapidly, and the increased use is moving up to college campuses.

College women have long faced the peril of date rape, sometimes abetted by use of alcohol or other date-rape drugs. But a new drug—Rohypnol—is even more effective for the rapist, and increases the danger for college women. It is tasteless, colorless, and odorless, and it dissolves quickly in drinks. It causes amnesia, paralysis of extremities, and loss of inhibitions for up to twelve hours. A person can participate in sex without voluntarily doing so, and not remember it afterward. And experts say Rohypnol is available on most campuses for only one or two dollars a pill. The threat posed by Rohypnol was thought to be so great that former President Clinton signed a bill in early October of 1996 that called for penalties of up to twenty years in prison for possession of Rohypnol to commit a crime. Later that same month, four Clemson University students were arrested for possession of Rohypnol.

"The law might put teeth into current laws against drugs used in rape, but too often date rape goes unreported and unprosecuted," said psychologist Mary Koss of the University of Arizona. "Date rapes," she continued, "are often considered minor crimes when they occur on college campuses, and are not vigorously investigated."

Sexual Promiscuity

Sexual relations, whether prompted by alcohol, other drugs, peer pressure, or consensual desires, are a major conduct factor on college campuses, with all the attendant problems of sexually transmitted disease, unwanted pregnancies, etc.

Violence

Officials at the American Medical Association say drinking not only affects students' health, but also causes increases in violence, personal injuries, property damage, acquaintance rape, and low grades.

The Columbia study reported that 95 percent of all violent crime on campus is alcohol related.

Dr. LaLance indicated that arguments and conflicts on campus are much more likely to result in violence than was the case several decades ago, and weapons—primarily guns and occasionally knives—are sometimes utilized in "conflict resolution." Four students at one university in the 20,000-enrollment range were murdered in separate incidents last year.

Cheating

Cheating on examinations and writing assignments is rampant on college campuses, obviously indicating a stronger student concern for grades and credentials than for learning.

A number of studies have found that more than two-thirds of college students are guilty of engaging in some form of academic dishonesty, and it is increasing, with much of the increase among women.

Professor Donald L. McCabe of Rutgers University has done extensive research and conducted many studies on academic dishonesty by students. In 1993 he explained: "As many as 20 percent of college students will cheat, no matter what we do. And 20 percent will never cheat, no matter what we do. We're fighting for that 60 percent in between. . . . If, as freshmen they see upperclassmen are not cheating, they tend to go in that direction; but if they see widespread cheating, they'll probably join the cheaters."

Cheating in intercollegiate athletics is also common. Coaches and institution officials sometimes tamper with an athlete's credentials, enabling him or her to qualify for admission; and special inducements—money, a car, a job for a parent or relative, etc.—are sometimes offered to a prized potential recruit. In order to make or keep an athlete eligible, faculty sometimes make grade concessions.

In August of 1996, criminal justice professors Frank Cullen and Edward Latessa of the University of Cincinnati conducted what was primarily a gambling investigation funded by the National Collegiate Athletic Association. Of 2,000 male Division I basketball and football players, 648 responded. Two-thirds indicated they had broken NCAA rules, one-quarter admitted to betting on athletic events, and a fraction said they had taken money from gamblers to control their performance in games.

Outlaw Athletes

"Cheered on Saturday afternoons and arrested on Saturday night, outlaw athletes are everywhere. On the East Coast, the West Coast and points in between. At large schools and small ones." This is the lead paragraph of a Hal Bock Associated Press story printed in newspapers in late November of 1996. For example, it was printed in the *Standard Times* of New Bedford, Massachusetts, in that month under the title "Field of Crimes."

Bock explains that nearly every day some player somewhere is charged with some offense, not run-of-the-mill NCAA violations, but misdemeanors and felonies—gambling, assault, theft, and rape. And in 2000 the stories continue and increase in number and severity. Bock illustrates:

> Last week five members of the Southwestern Michigan basketball team were charged with raping an 18-year-old female student and videotaping the act. The players, all freshmen, were expelled after their arraignment and could face life in prison if convicted.
>
> During one particularly ugly weekend last month, four Texas Christian football players were suspended following an assault, a Southern California running back was charged with rape, and a Virginia Tech wide receiver was dismissed from the team after being charged with shoplifting.
>
> During the same weekend, the University of Rhode Island threw two players off the team, suspended four others and forfeited its next game to punish 31 members of the football team allegedly involved in an attack on a fraternity.

Apparently a band of football players invaded the Theta Delta Chi fraternity and beat three members severely enough to send them to the hospital. The players broke windows and doors and terrorized fraternity members, reportedly because two players were refused entry to a party.

University President Robert Carothers ordered URI's next game—against Connecticut—forfeited, the first time in NCAA history that a university president had taken such action because of players' behavior.

Theft

Students need to be continually alert to the possibilities of theft, which is a major problem on many campuses. Books and items of clothing such as jackets and hats, if left unattended for even a few minutes in a public place such as a dining hall, student center, or a library, can quickly disappear and be sold by a thief.

Carelessness about securing a dormitory room can lead to the loss of more expensive items, such as electronic equipment.

UNIVERSITY CONDUCT

Some university presidents turn their backs on campus-community problems and pretend they don't exist, while others point to the demise of the in loco parentis concept (the institution assumed a role similar to that of parents for the students it enrolled) as rendering them virtually powerless to be intrusive in the campus environment.

Universities today can't be expected to return to the practices of the first American colleges in which a teacher had the responsibility for the total development—intellectual, moral, spiritual, and social—of a group of students for the students' four-year college experience, and the learning-supportive environment consisted of the teacher living with the students around the clock.

Nor can universities go back to the in loco parentis conditions of a number of decades ago when colleges dominated students and the campus environment.

A strong set of policies, regulations, and exhortations from above (the university) will not by themselves suffice, although a strong stand by the university is important to undergird a total program. But there are other things a university can do to help establish a learning-supportive campus environment, such as the following:

Radical Recommendation 62
Dealing with the Alcohol Problem

Assess your campus alcohol problem; develop a plan to deal with it, involving all segments of the campus; empower students to take the lead; and vigorously enforce alcohol policies.

Henry Wechsler in his 1996 *Change* article suggests a twelve-step program to deal with campus alcohol problems. Among his suggestions are:

- Thoroughly assess the problem in your university or college.
- Turning the problem over to a dean or a vice president for student affairs will not suffice. The problem is campus-wide, and developing a solution will require the active leadership of the president.
- Develop a long-range plan. Change won't come easily or quickly.
- Involve all campus segments in the solution—student government and other students, student service personnel, faculty and staff with expertise in the area, campus police, resident advisors, and athletic department personnel and athletes.
- Most important: empower students to take the lead. A successful and sustainable effort depends on the extent to which students are seen as the leaders of their own self-generated code of respectful community behavior—or the targets of it. The aim is to make drunkenness an unacceptable excuse for violent and disruptive behavior that violates other students' rights.
- Protect nonbinge drinkers. By focusing on protecting those who suffer from the second-hand effects of binge drinking, an institution could mobilize great numbers of students to assert their rights to live free from the annoyance and physical harm that stem from the alcohol abuse of others.
- Vigorously enforce alcohol policies.
- Confront binge drinking at fraternities and sororities.
- Show caring for problem drinkers by providing them with counseling and encouraging them to seek help or treatment.
- In freshman orientation, long before students arrive on campus, send the message loud and clear: We do not offer a major in binge drinking!

- Providing alcohol-free as well as other substance-free dormitory options is a partial solution already being offered on some campuses.

Radical Recommendation 63
Drugs and Sex

Education about drugs, especially Rohypnol, and about contraception and sexually transmitted diseases should be provided by the college or the university.

Most other harmful drugs are illegal, but each campus should still have a program to deal with them, centered around drug education. The importance of education is heightened by the easy availability of drugs including Rohypnol, on many campuses. Rohypnol is tasteless, colorless, and odorless, and it dissolves quickly in a drink. It renders a woman powerless to resist rape, and she will not remember the incident after the effects of the drug wear off. The only protection a woman has against Rohypnol is her knowledge about the drug and the continuous vigilance of her drinks that knowledge will prompt.

Education is also the key to dealing with problems associated with sexual promiscuity—education about contraception, sexually transmitted diseases, and values.

Violence

As for the problems of violence, since 95 percent of violence on campus is alcohol related, an effective alcohol abuse program will be a deterrent to violence.

In addition, because violence and other serious conduct problems, many of them criminal in nature, seem to be swirling around athletic departments, as indicated in the section titled "Outlaw Athletes," it would seem wise to turn to athletic programs first in a search for solutions to serious campus conduct problems.

Initially, let's look at the athletes. Who are the universities letting in to play football and basketball?

Football is a violent sport played by very aggressive people. Most football coaches know that if they do not recruit sometimes violent, aggressive players, their teams won't win and they will lose their jobs. Basketball is often violent—"physical"—also, especially under the basket.

Athletes are not just "let in"; they are usually aggressively recruited and they expect to be revered for their capabilities. These are often people who grew up having rules broken for them, people who are socially undisciplined. They often have trouble fitting into a student body with which they have little in common.

Then these athletes are placed under tremendous pressure. The primary thing expected of them is to perform at the highest possible level in their sport—to win. They will spend a great deal of time at practice sessions, viewing films, studying plays, working out in weight rooms, being treated for injuries in the training room, traveling to and from games and missing classes, and trying to study for their classes while exhausted from practice or a game, or when they are so "pumped up" for the next game that concentrating on their studies becomes extremely difficult or impossible.

There should be efforts to lessen pressures on athletes, but without lowering conduct or academic standards for them.

There should be concern shown to athletes as individuals. For example, as an aftermath of athlete-conduct problems at the University of Tennessee, the university established the Unity Council, a group of senior players who meet with head football coach Phillip Fulmer on a regular basis to discuss concerns about teammates.

As Donald L. McCabe reports in his studies on academic dishonesty, former quarterback Peyton Manning explained: "It's a way for Coach Fulmer to know what's going on with the team. He'll say, 'Guys, anybody with any problems?' We might say, 'This guy is hanging around with the wrong people. You might want to talk to him.' Nobody's telling on the guy, but otherwise Coach Fulmer has no way of knowing."

The council then becomes a tool for Fulmer to rescue players, pull them back from the brink of trouble.

Another way to avoid conduct problems is, in the recruiting process, look not only for good athletic ability, but also for good academic ability and good character.

Finally, because of their high visibility on campus, encourage coaches and prominent athletes to play leading roles in a continuing program for sensible and responsible conduct.

ALL CATEGORIES OF CAMPUS
CONDUCT PROBLEMS

The key to finding solutions to all student conduct problems presented in this chapter is the involvement of students in discussing the problems, establishing conduct standards and rules, and enforcing the rules.

Earlier in this chapter, in regard to campus alcohol problems, Wechsler suggested that all segments of the campus be involved in seeking solutions, and that students be empowered to take the lead, emphasizing the protection of nonbinge drinkers, and counseling, treatment, and rehabilitation of problem drinkers.

In regard to cheating, Professor McCabe, through his extensive research on academic dishonesty by students, came to the following conclusion: "Student behavior can be influenced by campus environment, especially when students are given significant authority and responsibilities to influence their peers."

Honor codes illustrate this point. Various aspects of the honor code at the University of Virginia are regularly debated and voted upon by the student body, and this has strengthened the UV code. Institutions with honor codes, if emphasized to students before they enroll at a college and during attendance as well, have significantly less cheating than institutions without honor codes.

During the late 1960s, student protest raged across campuses nationally, sometimes erupting into building takeovers, damage to and destruction of facilities, injuries, and even death to individuals. Reasons for the protest were multiple, and needed to be variously addressed.

In addition to national military policy and racial and gender concerns, students at Middle Tennessee State University were concerned about campus rules and regulations and their application by the university. The university formed a rules committee composed of a number of students and a few faculty members and student personnel officers. The committee met annually to discuss rules and recommend changes that were deemed improvements. A student court system, capped by a Student Supreme Court, was developed for rule implementation. This system worked well over the years and is still in effect.

Radical Recommendations 64–65
Campus Environment: Curricular Help

64. Develop a core course about comparative religions.
65. Develop a core course in values, ethics, and morals.

A core course about religions should be developed, from which some students will adopt basic tenets that will guide their campus conduct in positive ways.

A core course on values, ethics, and morals will undoubtedly have a similar positive effect on some students.

While such courses can be helpful, college officials should recognize that in regard to student conduct and values, students are going to be influenced at least as much by what academics do as by what they say. Academics should, therefore, conduct themselves accordingly.

Students will note the hypocrisy in college catalogs and other publications which describe the wonderful things the institution will do for its students, and which the institution then not only falls far short of producing, but does not even make a serious effort to produce.

Students will also often be aware of corruption in athletic programs where it exists. And students will be disillusioned by professors in the classroom who are unfair or who even debunk traditional values. An example of the latter:

A professor in a freshman foreign language course returned graded midterm essay examination papers to a class, and then proceeded to discuss each question with the class. As he was discussing the next to last question, a male student raised his hand, and upon gaining recognition, said, "Sir, I omitted this question, and you didn't deduct any points from my grade for the omission." The professor responded, "Well, Mr. Boy Scout, bring me the paper and I'll lower the grade right now." For the remainder of the class and in class for several weeks thereafter, the professor continued to derisively refer to the student as the "Boy Scout," mocking his honesty.

Nonconduct Recommendations

A non-student-conduct factor inhibiting large institutions from developing a collegial, learning-supportive campus environment is sheer size of student bodies, some numbering forty thousand or more. Still, advantages of a supportive environment are many, and warrant serious exploration of possible means to that end, several of which were discussed in the chapter on the academic program.

Although it would be ideal, it is likely physically impossible to divide most universities into a number of small, related colleges à la Cambridge and Oxford, campuses that were initially designed for such division.

In the Claremont University Center in California, five small colleges and a graduate school operate in a somewhat loose cluster system. They share in the financial benefit of the large, joint operation, while providing the interactive educational and social atmosphere of the small college.

The Iowa Plan seems much more attainable and has great potential. It consists of forming groups of students who will be enrolled together in some general education classes for the first couple of years. Going to class together can provide a unifying intellectual and social life like that students get in small colleges.

Dr. Donald N. McClosky of the University of Iowa says that students so grouped begin to do intellectual work in common; they study together, they end up in this collegial atmosphere thinking together about what they've learned together.

McClosky suggests that the housing office could assign people in the same academic group to the same dormitory. He concludes: "We can create 30 or 40 small colleges out of one immense one, at no additional cost." This would be a giant step toward the creation of a collegial, learning-supportive environment.

At Michigan State University in the 1960s, a plan was developed to provide coherence and support for freshmen students. In one building were dormitory rooms, a dining hall, classrooms, and offices of faculty who taught freshmen courses. When not in class, the faculty were in their offices and available to provide assistance to students, and trained counselors lived in the building to help students after the end of the faculty work day.

Sounds a little like the early American colleges, in which students received around-the-clock attention.

Lifetime Conduct

Some of the suggestions in the preceding sections of this chapter, for example, those about alcohol and drug education for a better campus atmosphere, will be helpful in developing lifetime character and values. Also, courses on religions and values can have much broader implications than helping to create a more learning-friendly campus environment.

For example, look at a required core course about religions. In learning about religions, some students will find basic tenets that will help them become better people and help develop a kinder, more fair, more caring society.

By learning more about religions, students can become more understanding and more tolerant of different religions. And they can seek commonalities among religions and help people of different faiths to seek commonalities, and to emphasize these instead of differences.

Developing tolerance and emphasizing commonalities could help lessen tensions and conflict between those of the many different faiths in American society. And surely it would help protect the 6 million Muslims living in America from the kind of stigmatization and persecution many Japanese-Americans suffered during World War II.

A required course in the core about religions is a must!

If institutions are to concentrate on the development of the whole student, great emphasis must be placed on values. It should be understood that neither institutionally mandated values, ethics, and morality, nor their presentation in lectures is likely to influence many students to develop strong values, ethics, and morals.

John Stuart Mill argued that freedom of expression needed to be protected so that our most cherished values could be questioned, enlivened, reaffirmed, or transformed in the crucible of debate.

Willimon and Naylor in *The Abandoned Generation* in 1995 say: "Values must not only be 'clarified,' they must be debated, judged, exemplified, demonstrated, and tested before the young if they are to be embraced by and inculcated in the young."

Values, then, should be studied and debated in class (in a required core course) and outside of class, with the understanding that all will not develop the exact same value system, but all will have engaged in serious study, debate, and deliberation about values, and each will have developed a system with which he or she feels comfortable—a system that he or she will then likely incorporate into his or her life.

In addition to a course on values, a campus must establish its own values and model the values it espouses, because students will be affected by what they see as well as by what they hear.

Finally, as another way to assist in the education and development of the whole student, and better meet society's needs, the Wingspread report recommends that "universities wholeheartedly commit themselves to providing students with opportunities to experience and reflect on the world beyond the campus. . . . Academic work should be complemented by the kinds of knowledge derived from first-hand experience, such as contributing to the well-being of others, participating in political campaigns, and working with the enterprises that create wealth in our society."

The benefits of experiential service learning are strongly presented by Alexander Astin, one of the premier researchers and thinkers on higher education, in an Eisenhower Leadership essay in 1996.

> Recent studies conducted by the Higher Education Research Institution show clearly participation in service activities during the undergraduate years has beneficial effects on students' academic development, sense of civic responsibility, and life skills (including leadership skills). It also has a number of positive effects on students' post-college development. . . . [C]ourse-based service learning . . . represents a potentially powerful tool for integrating good educational practice into the curriculum. . . . [S]ervice learning gives us an opportunity to combine, in one activity, many of the educational techniques and practices that recent research on teaching and learning has shown to be highly effective:
>
> - student involvement
> - collaborative learning
> - a common curricular experience
> - reflection
> - active learning
> - interdisciplinary studies
> - experiential learning
> - laboratory or field experience

Getting students involved in altruistic service activities—helping others—will likely enable many students to gain the insight discovered by many in the Peace Corps and Habitat for Humanity, namely: "You can't sprinkle the perfume of happiness on others without getting some on yourself."

Radical Recommendation 66
The Problem of Size

Large institutions should seek solutions to the problem of size as they wrestle with the many problems of providing a learning-supportive campus environment for students.

Radical Recommendation 67
The "Whole Student"

Universities and colleges should concentrate on the education and development of the whole student through various ways, such as: providing a required core course on religions, providing a core course on values, and providing the opportunities for significant experiential learning on and off campus.

ADDENDUM

Since material was initially gathered for this book, there has been a continual increase in the severity of the problems discussed. For example, alcohol-related arrests on college campus surged 24.3 percent in 1998, the largest jump in seven years, according to a survey by the *Chronicle of Higher Education.*

The results of the survey, released in mid-June of 2000 and based on the most recent statistics available, showed an 11.1 percent increase in college campus arrests for drug violations and an 11.3 percent increase in arrests for forcible sex offenses, as well as smaller increases in arrests for weapons violations, assault, arson, and hate crimes.

A survey released in 2000 by the Harvard School of Public Health found 22.7 percent of the college student population reported frequent binge drinking in 1999, up from 19.8 in 1993 and 20.9 percent in 1997. The survey included fourteen thousand students at 119 colleges.

Henry Wechsler, director of the recent and earlier Harvard college student alcohol studies, said, "Colleges do have traditions where drinking is part of their culture, and that needs to be changed."

These brief updates emphasize the escalating seriousness of the campus conduct problems which must be effectively addressed if proposed college and university educational reform is to enable the institutions to provide vastly improved educational opportunities for students.

Some will say that the increasing decadence of the student culture on many campuses is simply a reflection of the decline and decadence in the overall society, and while there is some truth to that observation, that does not justify universities tolerating such student cultures.

Nor does it excuse universities' neglect of religions, values, and off-campus service activities.

Reengineering the campus environment, emphasizing values and the study of religions, and developing programs of interaction with the off-campus community will enable a university to achieve a primary goal—improving the knowledge, skills, and character of its students, and producing graduates who will be better than the society they enter, and who will influence its improvement.

Such university achievement is a major source of hope for a better America in the twenty-first century.

FOURTEEN

FINANCES

YESTERDAY AND TOMORROW

For more than the last two decades, the American economy has been in a roller coaster mode. The recession of the late 1980s and early 1990s was followed by an upturn in the economy in the mid-1990s that lasted for about six years. Now in the early years of the new millennium, we are witnessing another economic downturn, the extent of which is yet to be determined.

How did American businesses, organizations, and higher education respond to the frightening problems of the recession?

Corporate and civic leaders interview in 1995 studies by the California Higher Education Policy Center and the American Council on Education "felt that businesses and many other institutions in this country have gone through a painful process of restructuring over the last twenty years. As difficult as the process has been, many of those interviewed believe it often has been a healthy one, and that these organizations are doing a better job at lower cost. *The consensus is that higher education has not even begun the restructuring process, and that it has not succeeded in getting costs under control.*" This is a quote from the article "What the Public Thinks of Colleges" by John Immerwahr and James Harvey in the March 12, 1995, issue of the *Chronicle of Higher Education.*

Other evidence seems to support the conclusions presented in the Immerwahr-Harvey article. Thus, the early 1990s recession and near panic about higher education finances extended to the mid-1990s, when a six-year period of prosperity began. While some steps toward financial reform in higher education were begun, the healthy status of colleges and universities was almost certainly more the result of a revitalized economy than of financial reform within higher education.

Instead of undergoing stringent self-analysis, restructuring, and downsizing during the last two decades, many universities have continued their financially irresponsible growth. They have failed to diligently seek cost effectiveness in their institutions. Instead they raised the tuition of undergraduates as much as 50 percent over a five-year period.

Even worse, they surreptitiously used money from high undergraduate tuition to support graduate schools and research, from which the undergraduate rarely received any direct benefit, according to the Boyer Commission report.

What we have here is universities socking it to their undergraduates in the form of high tuition instead of diligently seeking solutions to their severe financial problems.

This is another illustration of the rip-off of undergraduates by their universities!

GOING BACK IN TIME

With another recession possibly lurking around the corner in 2003, it would seem wise to prepare for it by learning what we can from the recession of the late 1980s and the early 1990s. Instead of just looking back, it would seem more helpful to place outselves back into that recession period to examine the ideas and proposals of state officials and educators to deal with higher education's financial exigencies of the times. What were their discussions like then?

An Atmosphere of Panic Begins to Appear in the Early 1990s

The severity of the financial crisis was emphasized by not only the decrease of initial state appropriations, but also the necessity of making mid-year cuts in already bare-bones budgets. The April 28, 1993, *Chronicle of Higher Education* reported that twenty states made mid-year cuts in their public colleges' budgets in 1992–93.

In the October 27, 1993, issue of the *Chronicle* it was stated that states were providing their colleges 2 percent more money in 1993–94 than they did two years before. The study which produced those figures calculated percentage change over two-year periods.

The study report continued that the gain was slight and that the 1993–94 2 percent increase concealed states that were still struggling with budget cuts.

Further, the report in the *Chronicle* stated that "when the 1993–94 figures are adjusted for inflation, colleges in 29 states have less buying power than two years ago, while those in four others have no increase. . . . [And in states] where gains were small, colleges may still face budget cuts."

While minuscule gains have been made recently, the national financial forecast for state institutions is far from sunny, said Kit Lively in the July 14, 1993, issue of the *Chronicle*.

A slight increase in President Clinton's 1995 budget would restore the largest Pell Grant award to $2,400, up from $2,300.

This would be of some small help to students facing tuition rates that were climbing more than 6 percent a year.

Because of the increase in costs, student borrowing was going up in what has been described as a "borrowing blitz."

Indiana official Jim Zook said in the April 27, 1994, issue of the *Chronicle* that the experiences on Indiana campuses are representative of the trend. Indiana students borrowed "60 million this year—an increase of almost 38 percent above the total for the previous year. . . ." And more than fifty-four hundred additional students sought loans that year compared to the 1992–93 number.

Seniors, many of whom had no job prospects, were greatly concerned about the size of the debts they had accumulated, said Zook in the *Chronicle*.

Voluntary support for higher education is a natural focus during times of financial exigency, but colleges said they had to fight harder and harder—and smarter—for donations.

The 1993 report of the Council for Aid to Education indicated that: "Colleges received $11.2 billion in private donations in 1992–93, 4.7 more than they raised a year earlier. But adjusted for inflation, the increase was just 1.5 percent—in a year when spending for operations, also adjusted for inflation, increased by 3 percent."

Approaches in the 1990s to State Financial Crises

The recession and attendant panic of the early 1990s prompted drastic responses from external (to higher education institutions) bodies such as legislatures, coordinating boards, and governing boards, as they sought to provide for the states' higher education needs with declining resources.

Massachusetts and several other states, faced with increasing costs of providing the various state services and decreased state revenues, opted to cut the seemingly astronomical costs of state higher education by diminishing the role of some state universities. The initial target was regional universities, each of which provided a full range of undergraduate programs and some general graduate programs for residents within a reasonable proximity of the institution.

Some governors and legislators said that the only way they could provide quality higher education was to cut the quantity of programs offered. Massachusetts moved ahead to force much more specialization on seven regional public colleges, and eliminate many of the similar basic programs from most of the seven campuses.

James Appleberry, president of the American Association of State Colleges and Universities pointed out: "If the mission is so focused, then you are going to deny access to people who don't have the financial wherewithal to go to another part of the state."

The residences of those who major in a particular discipline would be largely clustered about the institution offering the specialized program.

The financial crunch prompted Mississippi to attempt even more drastic steps. The higher education board in Mississippi recommended combining two state institutions and eliminating some others. One of the institutions to be merged was a historically black institution (to be merged with a predominantly white institution), as was one recommended for closing. The courts considered the charge of racial inequity in the proposal.

The Illinois Board of Higher Education responded to the state's financial crunch by developing a plan called "Priorities, Quality, and Productivity," the purpose of which was to channel scarce resources into high priorities for the state, according to an article in the May 25, 1994, issue of the *Chronicle of Higher Education*: "The Board asked campuses to reallocate 6 to 8 percent of their budgets over three years, starting in 1993. . . . Programs were to be considered for elimination if they had academic problems, high costs, or low enrollments, or if they were peripheral to a university's mission."

Monies were to be transferred from eliminated programs to identified high priorities, which included strengthening undergraduate teaching and keeping college affordable, priorities with which few could disagree.

During the recession of the early 1990s, layoffs became commonplace, and in spite of a slight economic upturn, the layoffs continued as colleges made selective cuts and adopted long-term strategies to contain costs.

"Colleges are aiming their knives at personnel because the costs of salaries, health benefits, and retirement packages account for as much as 70 or 80 percent of their operating budgets," says Julie L. Nicklin in the May 6, 1994, issue of the *Chronicle*. Nicklin continues, "New England College . . . is trying to erase a $1-million deficit by reducing its full-time faculty to 48 from 66."

MIT was facing a $10-million deficit in its operating budget of $350 million and Bill Dickson, senior vice president, said that MIT was at least four hundred staff people too big. The planned reduction, he said, "would come through layoffs, attrition, and buyouts and early retirement." Dickson said that MIT was in the process of "re-engineering" itself to handle administrative tasks with greater cost effectiveness.

In two waves of cuts since 1990, Stanford University laid off about 280 staff workers and administrators to save $65 million. It then wanted to cut an additional $20 million from its $469-million operating budget over the next three years by laying off up to one hundred middle- and upper-level managers and staff workers.

These are just a few examples of an apparent trend to cut costs by reductions in personnel.

Responses to the Problem of Rising Student Costs

Before 1990 and during the "panic years" of the early 1990s, costs to students shot up at an alarming rate, causing many observers to express the fear that the rising costs would make college unavailable to large numbers of otherwise qualified potential students.

In response to this problem, Georgia Governor Zell Miller proposed a lottery-funded student-grant program.

"Governor Miller wants his state to cover the full tuition at public colleges and universities for good students from families with incomes of up to $100,000," said Joyce Mercer in the November 3, 1993, *Chronicle of Higher Education.*

This was to be an expansion of a fledgling program that already paid the tuition of college freshmen and sophomores with "B" averages and family incomes up to $66,000.

"The awards are known as HOPE Grants, for 'Helping Outstanding Pupils Educationally. . . . Governor Miller . . . proposed the HOPE program in September 1992. Getting it off the ground was contingent on voters' approval of a statewide lottery, which they gave a year ago. Lawmakers then passed the grant program this year. . . . It appears that Georgia can afford to expand the program. Lottery players have bought more than $300 million in tickets since the sales began on June 29," said Gwen L. Hopkins, press secretary for the Georgia Lottery Corporation.

Sales of $460 million were projected for the first full year, and with $300 million in the coffers after only four months of sales, it appeared that the goal was well within reach.

The program has expanded on into the twenty-first century.

(I've presented information about the HOPE program, but I do not recommend it because of the grief it brings to the many who can't afford to play, but do so any way. However, Tennessee voters approved a lottery in November of 2002.)

Another plan provides financial help to students "down the road."

Prepayment of tuition programs have been gaining popularity in recent years. Tennessee began its Baccalaureate Education System Trust (BEST) in 1997, and by June 1998 more than three thousand had enrolled in the program.

BEST enables parents, grandparents, and others to keep inflation at bay by paying for a college education in advance. The plan allows the purchase of tuition units at today's rates ($24.50 per unit) for future students, even while they are infants.

The premise is that state money managers, accustomed to handling huge pension investments, can produce a return on the funds greater than the growth of college tuition costs. In Tennessee, pension fund investments have grown at a rate of 10.6 percent over the past decade while tuition rates have increased about 7 percent.

Beginning in the fall of 1999, money from the program could be used to pay for room and board as well as tuition. Also beginning in the fall of 1999, computer owners were able to dial up the state's Web site, download the full enrollment kit, print it out, sign it, and mail it back in.

Advantages of the BEST program were:

- BEST's flexibility lets participants decide when to save and how much to save.
- Tuition units can be used for college costs anywhere in the nation.
- Federal taxes are deferred on appreciation of the account until the units are used. At that point the income tax on the increase in value is calculated at the child's rate.
- The ability to purchase a few units at a time makes college costs more affordable.
- Saving through BEST frees participants from concerns about investment decisions.
- Saving through BEST helps the purchaser and the child avoid any temptation to spend college savings on other things.
- Enrollment in BEST encourages the child and friends and relatives to share in the college savings process.

RATIONAL RADICAL RECONSTRUCTIVE REFORM

Higher education must look within to find long-term solutions to its financial problems.

The comprehensive restructuring process mentioned in the California Higher Education Policy Center (C.H.E.P.C.) and ACE studies, and recommended in the Boyer Commission report (1998), the Wingspread report (1993), the several comparable studies in the 1980s, and the earlier recommendations of knowledgeable and prestigious groups are exemplified in Dr. Finn's "No Frills University" proposal.

Chester E. Finn Jr., former Assistant Secretary of Education, proposed a tough and comprehensive plan to counter the escalating costs of higher education and improve the education in the bargain. In the October 26, 1988, *Chronicle of Higher Education*, Finn lamented:

American higher education over all is needlessly expensive and getting more so. This is partly because competition has worked perversely.

Instead of vying to offer the best, trimmest product at the lowest possible price, colleges compete to erect elaborate facilities, to offer trendy new programs, and to dangle before prospective students the gaudiest array of special services, off-campus options, extra-curricular activities, snazzy dorms, and yuppified dining-hall menus.

There is more to the college price spiral, however, than colleges' tendency to add frills and furbelows. Most institutions are woefully inefficient, too. Facilities sit idle much of the time. The "academic year" usually consists of just a pair of 13-week semesters, and professors aren't expected to be around the other six months. Moreover, when present, they are apt to teach only a couple of courses at a time, maybe six to nine hours a week of classroom activity.

In the same article from the *Chronicle*, Finn proposes a "No-Frills University" to turn the higher-education marketplace upside down, so that colleges would "begin to compete in terms of efficiency, instructional quality, and low prices." According to Finn, there are eight features that would distinguish such an institution:

1. The college would have no assistant deans or associate vice-presidents and not much nonteaching staff. "Instead of hiring full-time grounds crews, dishwashers, and gym attendants, the college would expect 10 hours or so per week of service from its students. Jobs they could not handle would be contracted out to private vendors."
2. "Most quality-of-life amenities would be left to entrepreneurs. . . . Students would pay only for what they consumed."
3. The same principle would apply to college-provided services—employment offices, psychological counseling, the use of art studios and athletic facilities. Students would pay for what they used.
4. The college would operate year-round, on a four-quarter basis. Students could complete a bachelor's degree in three years. Facilities would be in constant use and employees would have steady work.
5. "The faculty would be well paid but would work hard. Nobody would have 'tenure'; renewable five-year contracts would be the norm. So would be teaching three or four courses per quarter. . . . [T]here would be no expectation that all faculty members would routinely do

research; instead, excellent teachers would be recruited and paid salaries from $50,000 to $100,000." (These figures are impressive when adjusted for fifteen years of inflation.)

6. "The college would have a rich and rigorous core curriculum, aimed at producing knowledgeable, clear-thinking adults acquainted with the central ideas of Western civilization and the principal ways of organizing and using knowledge." The core would count for about half of a student's total program of study, with the "major" occupying much of the rest.

7. Rigorous exit standards would mean that those who could not demonstrate the requisite skills and knowledge would get no diploma until they could do so.

8. Students would wind up paying different amounts depending on how many optional services they used, but they would all pay on the same basis.

Such a "no-frills university" could offer a student a good education for a fraction of the costs at a "country-club university."

Scarlett's Financial Recommendations

About thirty years ago, as a university president, I proposed a "fairness in tuition" plan to my governing board. The plan was simple: Do away with package tuition deals, and charge every student a flat rate for each credit hour taken.

The practice was, and still is, to charge a standard tuition fee to every full-time student, usually defined as a person taking a minimum of twelve hours a semester or quarter. Such a student would be allowed to take three, six, or sometimes even nine additional hours at no additional cost to the student. Part-time students—those taking fewer than twelve hours—were charged an amount for each credit hour taken. Multiplying a full-time student's credit hours by the per-hour rate showed that the full-time student was paying less per hour than the part-time student. The irony of this is that the part-time student often could take only a limited course load because he, lacking financial resources, often found it necessary to work full-time in order to afford to take only a few courses.

The part-time student with a limited ability to pay was in effect subsidizing the education of the full-time student who apparently had greater ability to pay.

But this inequity was not only a fairness issue. It was also a financial issue. A theoretical application of the per-hour-rate tuition charge to all students then enrolled, of course, showed that full-time students would pay more, thus providing a considerable income increase to the institution—in the name of fairness!

The board rejected the proposal.

The "fairness in tuition" plan, in which each student paid the same rate for what he or she received, was right in line with Finn's "No-Frills University" proposal.

In Finn's plan, instead of paying blanket fees for services and facilities, students would pay only for the specific services and facilities they used. This feature and Finn's other recommendations for a low-cost, quality education are similar to a number of the recommendations I made earlier in this volume.

Obviously, I think they are worthy of very serious consideration.

Obstacle #25
Increasing Financial Problems

Real long-term solutions to financial problems will have to come from within higher education. Less money means that colleges and universities are going to have to find more efficient, effective ways to operate.

Radical Recommendations 68–70
Providing More with Less

68. **Colleges and universities must be better managed. Doctoral programs should provide a course in college administration for those students who might like to become administrators, and colleges and universities should provide in-service training programs for administrators, especially department chairpersons.**

69. **Since faculty have often been reluctant to make tough cutback decisions, diminish the decision-making role of faculty in favor of**

a stronger role for academic administrators, as was suggested in recommendations 8 and 10.

70. **In a relentless quest for effective efficiency, there can be no sacred cows. Every aspect of the operation should be thoroughly scrutinized from the standpoint of: (1) Is it needed? (2) Is it effective? (3) Is it efficient?**

The following items, discussed in chapter 12, are examples of things which should be carefully examined: elimination of frivolous courses, consolidation of courses with considerable overlapping material, consolidation of duplicate courses in different departments (such as statistics), dropping of courses which continually have very small enrollments and are not essential to the program, scheduling essential courses with low enrollments less frequently, and seeking cooperative arrangements with other institutions for expensive foreign language programs.

All of the above could result in the saving of faculty costs. Nonfaculty positions should also be examined for fat which could be pared off. Gail Promboin points out that between 1975 and 1985, college and university administrative staffs grew 60 percent while faculties grew by 6 percent. During the same period, student costs grew by 30 percent above inflation. This looks suspiciously like administrative "empire building," and surely deserves careful study.

Then there is the matter of the possibility of unnecessary duplication of expensive programs between or among institutions. An extreme example would be the establishment of a second state-supported medical school in a state that was having great difficulty adequately supporting one medical school.

Obstacle #26
Resistance to Revision

The revision of an institution on the magnitude proposed by the Wingspread Group and the Boyer Commission will encounter tremendous difficulties as individuals and groups feel their "turf" is being invaded.

Without strong leadership from the president, backed by a staunchly supportive governing board, such a revision has little chance of success.

Radical Recommendation 71
Strengthen the Presidency

As recommended earlier, strengthen the college and university presidency. A good beginning would be to tender the president at least a several-year guaranteed contract.

Because of the massive perceived threat during World War II, the people of the United States pulled together in a tremendous national effort. A president who can develop a team spirit on campus even remotely comparable to that of World War II will have to be an outstanding leader and communicator. He must convince the campus community that the need for change is great, and that achieving major effective change is his problem, and their problem—all of them.

The president is going to need to have a strengthened position if he is going to lead an effort, in a system of institutions, to get the governing board to radically change the role of the system's central staff, which includes the chancellor, to whom the presidents report.

Radical Recommendation 72

As suggested earlier in chapter 6, change the role of central staff from administering the institutions to serving the needs of the governing board. Because of the vastly diminished role, the board can then slash the size of the staff, and distribute the considerable savings to the campuses for the educational program for students.

Radical Recommendations 73–77
Faculty

Altering the role of faculty can also produce a financial bonanza (in terms of teaching time) which can be used to reduce the size of large classes, reduce student tuition costs, and increase faculty salaries.

73. **Restore teaching to the dominant activity on most campuses, and place it on equal footing with research at research universities. (This item is repeated here because of its relevance to finances.)**

74. The pressure on all faculty to be productive, publishing researchers must be eliminated.

In his book *College,* Ernest Boyer reported that in Carnegie's survey of five thousand faculty members in four-year institutions, "63 percent reported that their interests 'lie toward teaching as opposed to research.'" . . . Even at research universities, almost 40 percent of the faculty showed a strong preference for teaching."

Obviously this indicates that more than 63 percent of the faculty at other than research universities prefer teaching over research.

If the campus reward system is altered, those who wish to teach full-time will be encouraged to do so.

75. Change the campus reward system so that top consideration for tenure, promotion, and salary increases can be earned by full-time teaching without extensive research productivity and publishing. (See recommendation 39.)

Over the years, faculty teaching loads have been reduced in order to give faculty time to do research and publish. If the faculty member no longer is expected to do considerable research and publishing, some of the reduced teaching load can be restored.

For example: At a college with one hundred faculty members, the teaching load is nine hours with the expectation that the faculty member will also research and publish. With the removal of that expectation, an additional course could be added to the load of each who chose to teach full-time. According to Boyer's survey, this would mean that at least sixty-three faculty members would teach an additional course, and the institution would get the equivalent of sixteen additional teachers.

This would enable the institution to reduce large classes and reduce faculty size, the savings from which could enable the college to reduce student tuition charges and increase faculty salaries.

76. Increase faculty teaching loads for those who choose not to do extensive research. (This item is repeated here because of its relevance to finances).

This will allow the faculty member to concentrate on his or her preference—teaching or research.

And it will allow the nonresearch faculty member to tap into the reward system at a high level, which he or she was unable to do when research productivity was the dominating factor.

The good reputation of the institution can be a significant factor in improving the institution's financial condition.

77. Use MBO and blueprint plans to improve teaching and the carrying out of institutional goals across campus. This is good education and good public relations. (This item is repeated here because of its relevance to finances).

More effective services will produce pleased customers—students, their parents, and graduates' employers. All will "spread the good word" about the institution, attracting more students (their fees and appropriations), and more donors.

Obstacle #27
Indifference to Student Needs

The great many colleges and universities that graduate only 50 percent, or even as low as 30 percent, of their students within five years after matriculation show a remarkable indifference to the welfare of their students.

It's true, as some will claim, that many students need to combine employment and their academic pursuits, so that it takes them longer than five years to earn a bachelor's degree. And it is equally true that other students drop out for personal reasons. But the overwhelming majority of students who do not earn a degree fail to do so because their institutions did not serve them well.

This point is aptly illustrated by the success of some institutions which have developed comprehensive retention programs, resulting in dramatic graduation-rate increases.

If a student satisfies an institution's admission requirements and is admitted, that institution has a moral responsibility to muster its resources to help the student succeed. And a successful retention program will provide a tremendous financial windfall for an institution.

If most of an institution's drop-outs occur during the freshman year, and a retention program is developed that cuts a 50 percent drop-out rate in half, the sophomore class will be increased by 25 percent. Most of those who have become acclimated and tasted success in the freshman year are likely to persist through to the sophomore, junior, and senior years.

When an institution has a large drop-out rate in the freshman year, many sophomore and especially junior and senior class sections become small. Thus, additional upperclassmen can be absorbed with little extra cost into the smaller classes.

Calculate the financial boon to the institution from the fees (and at state institutions, per-student appropriations also) of vastly increased numbers of sophomores, juniors, and seniors.

Radical Recommendation 78
Retention

Each institution should review retention-research results, examine successful retention programs at other colleges and universities, study the needs of their own students, and institute a thorough, comprehensive student retention program strongly backed by the president.

Obstacle #28
Ignoring Business Practices

It's true that higher education is very different from American businesses in significant ways. Basically, higher education is concerned with providing services, and the concern of businesses is making a profit. This is often the reason given by educators for not borrowing methods and procedures from business. But with the increasing need to get maximum benefit from the resources at its disposal, higher education can ill afford to ignore possibilities in business operations that might be useful in higher education.

Radical Recommendation 79
Business Practices

Higher education should leave no stone unturned in its quest for ways to perform its functions more efficiently and effectively. The process and methods of business should be carefully examined.

Eliminating course duplication and other wasteful practices, greatly increasing faculty productivity by increasing the teaching loads of faculty who prefer teaching to extensive research production, changing the role of board staffs and slashing their size, improving the efficiency and effectiveness of the services provided, and establishing an effective retention program will vastly increase college income and enable institutions to provide the improved and modernized services, and the lowered costs to students called for by the Wingspread Group.

There is still, however, a "sacred cow"—the academic calendar—which remains untouched. The inefficient calendar most in use consists of nine months—generally two semesters—of full course offerings, and a summer term in which only a sprinkling of courses is provided.

A resurrection of the tri-semester system, so highly touted several decades ago, for thorough consideration would seem to offer considerable benefit to students, colleges and universities, faculty, and taxpayers.

Such a system could enable students to earn a bachelor of arts degree in three or less years instead of the current four. It would bring in considerably more revenue to institutions through additional student fees and per-student appropriations in state universities. Faculties could work twelve months instead of nine, and their salaries could be increased accordingly.

Taxpayers would benefit as use of campus facilities became more cost effective when used the entire year instead of just nine months, and costs of new construction could be cut because current facilities could serve more students, lessening the need to provide additional buildings.

Radical Recommendation 80
A Sweeping Change

Seriously and thoroughly restudy the possible benefits, problems, and disadvantages in the establishment of a trimester calendar, with the full intent to institute such a system if the positives seem to outweigh the negatives.

PUBLIC RELATIONS AND PRIVATE FUND-RAISING

Another means of providing strong financial support for colleges and universities in the future is improving fund-raising. Moneys received from private sources might well be increased.

Independent colleges and universities already "work" the private sector hard. Many public colleges and universities might increase private giving to their institutions by working harder and smarter in this area.

Additional students can be another source of external income. With the upturn in the numbers of traditional-age students and the ready supply of older potential students, increasing enrollment provides excellent potential for increasing institutional income.

The other side of the coin—increasing external income through stepped-up gift-solicitation and student-recruitment programs—is also dependent on careful planning and activity within a college or university. Public relations is the key.

It is important to note that your college will be perceived in one way or another whether you consciously *work* at PR or not, but you may well be perceived in a negative, or at best a luke-warm light if you don't work at PR.

Communication is the primary activity of a PR program. In years past, a PR practitioner was principally engaged in transmitting information about his or her organization to its various publics through news releases, presentations, films, brochures, reports, etc. This was publicity. Now a vast number of organizations are recognizing that no amount of slick publicity is going to establish and long maintain good relations between their organizations and their various publics if the organization is not performing its basic functions effectively!

First comes good performance, then publicity, then good PR.

Public relations is now being perceived as a two-way communications process. The first way is publicity—transmitting information to its various publics. The second way is gathering information from the institution's publics about (a) how the public perceives the institution's performance, and (b) how the public perceives the PR program. The PR practitioner then relates the various publics' views on the institution's performance to top management so that management and faculty can reevaluate institutional performance and continually strive to improve it; and the PR director and staff reevaluate the publicity program with a view to improving it.

Such a continuous two-way communications process should enable an institution to establish and maintain good relations with its publics.

Reference has been made to an institution's publics. PR rarely deals with the general public, because the general public is made up of many differentiated publics. PR practitioners identify specific segmented groups of the general public, and relate to each group relative to the specific interests and concerns of the group.

Like most organizations, a college or a university has publics within the institution and outside the institution. Internal publics are students, faculty, administrators, and staff. External publics are alumni, parents of students, people in the immediate and extended community in which the university is located, local businesses and other businesses which are providers for the university, high school counselors, high school seniors, city, county, and staff officials, and so forth. For maximum effectiveness, then, a PR program will need to be both internal and external.

The president, with the assistance of the public relations expert, will play the major role in both internal and external public relations, but it should be understood that PR is also the responsibility of all in the college or university community, since all will benefit from the institution's effective public relations.

Summing up: public relations is simply doing a good job and getting credit for it. Project a favorable image of the college or university, and let it be a true image.

This is essential for effective fund-raising, effective student recruiting, effective student retention, and the long-term stability and significance of your college or university.

In *Troubled Times for American Higher Education* (1994), Clark Kerr pointed out that: "Average family real income after taxes for the top one percent income groups has gone up 136 percent from 1977 to 1992, while income for the other 99 percent has remained roughly constant; and this same one percent has had its tax bill reduced by $84 billion per in real dollars. This one percent has seemed to be willing to share its enormous gains by way of gifts to private colleges and universities, and this helps to explain the great success of many of their endowment campaigns."

Maximum potential for a college in fund-raising is not likely to be achieved by college staff alone. Volunteers should also be used.

Volunteers in fund-raising (or in student recruitment) programs provide a depth of credibility that college staff may not be able to offer because volunteers act without direct self-interest. They believe in the college's mission and in the effectiveness of the college in carrying out the mission.

Volunteers should be sought who have commitment, ability, influence, respect in the community, time, persistence, and ability to relate effectively to others. Affluence wouldn't hurt either.

Remember, 80 percent of the gifts to colleges are given by 20 percent or less of the donors. Fund raisers say it usually takes as much time to get a $500 gift as it does to get a $5,000 gift. So work on your biggest gift possibilities first. David R. Dunlap says that major gift givers are likely to have had experiences that caused them to become aware of that institution, to develop knowledge of it, and through increasing concern and caring involvement, to become committed to it. All of this is carefully orchestrated by the college. Major gift donors give their largest gifts to institutions with which they are closely and frequently involved, often over long periods of time.

The initial goal is to identify persons with the greatest financial capacity. Then do initial research on prospects to estimate gift size potential. Know the prospect as a whole person, and relate the prospect to your fund-raising goals. A cultivation calendar should be developed to coordinate planned college activities with the known interests of the prospects. Remember, court your prospects continually, not just when you want a contribution.

PART THREE
WRAPPING IT ALL UP

CONCLUSION

ACTION!

The eminent higher education authority Clark Kerr wrote in *Higher Education Cannot Escape History* (1994): "The United States has, overall, the most effective system of higher education the world has ever known." His reference to the world-leading accomplishments in research, professional schools, graduate schools, and unprecedented broad access is defensible, except in the area of the preparation of college teachers in U.S. graduate schools. However, he does not include undergraduate education in his laudatory assessment, as elsewhere he has written, "I have long been concerned with the declining quality of education for undergraduates in the United States. . . ."

His concerns about undergraduate education in the 1990s have been shared and expressed by other experts. And because of the snail's pace of change in higher education, many of the criticisms and recommendations for improvement presented during the last several decades are still relevant, providing a mountain of evidence and expert opinion on the outrageous neglect and malpractice primarily in undergraduate education. The rip-off of undergraduates continues.

In fairness it must be pointed out that there are still four-year institutions that place their major emphasis on promoting student learning, and in virtually all other colleges and universities there are many faculty who exhibit strong concern for the learning and development of their students. But they are swimming upstream against an ever-stronger current of homogenization generated by the thrust of most institutions to emulate the prestigious research universities.

LONG-STANDING CONCERNS

Most issues of concern expressed in this book are long-standing, and many studies and thoroughly developed recommendations concerning the issues have been presented primarily to higher education practitioners through presentations at professional meetings, scholarly books, specialized magazines, and especially the *Chronicle of Higher Education*, a weekly newspaper whose target readership is the academic community. Any alert administrator or faculty member can hardly fail to have been aware of the studies and the recommendations. Still, the studies and the recommendations were either ignored or their effect on colleges and universities has been nearly imperceptible.

Supporting this assessment is the fact that the reports and recommendations of the 1980s had little discernible effect on undergraduate education, as the problems and concerns they dealt with were still largely the problems and concerns of the 1990s.

And the trend continues into 2000, as the hard-hitting *An American Imperative: Higher Expectations for Higher Education* (1994) is apparently gathering dust on the back shelves of the relative few who acquired it. This is in spite of the dire consequences it predicted for U.S. society if the book's recommendations for sweeping undergraduate reform were not implemented.

The seeming resistance to change becomes more apparent as the history of some of the issues affecting undergraduate education is briefly traced, some even decades before the 1980s. Note the following:

The Presidency

An article in a July 1995 *Chronicle of Higher Education* presents one of the most glaring illustrations of higher education disinterest or even disdain for the thorough explorations of higher education's problems and the thoughtfully crafted recommended solutions.

Clark Kerr, the story said, headed a panel in 1980 for the Association of Governing Boards to examine the college and university presidency. The resulting study, described as the most intense to ever explore the subject, was full of sage advice for boards and presidents, emphasizing the importance of presidential leadership and structuring the conditions of the presidency to facilitate effective leadership. *Presidents Make a Difference*, the report of the panel, was largely ignored.

In announcing the appointment of a new panel ten years later to explore the same issues, Tom Ingram, president of the Association of Governing Boards of Universities and Colleges, explained: "So many of the concerns that Kerr identified have not gone away. Some of them have gotten worse." He said he could not identify even one recommendation from Kerr's report that had been carried out.

Preparation for College Teaching

In 1954 fifteen distinguished college and university teachers and administrators were assembled by the Fund for the Advancement of Education to study critical problems of graduate schools. After extensive surveying of relevant constituencies, thorough study, and dialogue, they issued a report, *The Graduate School Today and Tomorrow*, which said, in part, that the Ph.D. degree is not a teaching degree, that it does not certify, and was not created to certify teaching ability.

The report continues: "There should be established another doctor's degree, not less rigorous, but different. . . . [T]his degree should be directed toward preparing men and women to teach effectively in college."

It was almost fifteen years before any discernible response to the recommendation was seen. In the late 1960s and early 1970s, the Doctor of Arts degree was introduced at Carnegie Mellon and several other universities. It featured more breadth than the Ph.D., the interrelatedness of knowledge, pedagogy, and a somewhat lessened and different emphasis on research.

It is a degree to prepare college teachers, but it hasn't caught on, some say because of elitism and the prestige of the Ph.D. The D.A. in 1996 was found in a limited number of academic areas in only twenty-one universities.

Many have called for graduate schools to provide students with preparation for college teaching, including K. Patricia Cross, president of the American Association of Higher Education in the mid-1980s, and Ernest Boyer, culminating in his 1990 book *Scholarship Reconsidered*.

Still, more than forty years after the recommendation of the Committee of Fifteen, there appears to be very little preparation for college teaching provided by our graduate schools.

While the ripples being generated by the "Preparing Future Faculty Project" described in chapter 7 are encouraging, at this point it doesn't appear that they will be a major part of a tidal wave of reform that will sweep across U.S. campuses.

Teaching

With little preparation for college teaching being provided in graduate schools, it is little wonder that Pat Cross, then President of the American Association of Higher Education, would write in one of the association's 1986 bulletins:

> If Sleeping Beauty had dozed off in class at the University of Bologna in the 12th Century and been awakened recently by all of the noise about educational excellence, she would have awakened to a classroom that was quite familiar to her. Generations of students and teachers have come and gone; the printing press has made knowledge easily available to the masses; television producers have learned to disdain the "talking head"; computers offer new opportunities for interactive learning; but the talking head continues to reign supreme in higher education. So far "teaching as telling" has withstood the test of time.

In a 1993 essay in another AAHE bulletin, Wellesley College trustee Estelle Tanner also plays the historical theme, indicating that "American classrooms, to date, remain remarkably immune to change."

Technology in Instruction

Perhaps the rejection by college faculty of the growing knowledge of how students learn, effective teaching techniques, and use of educational technology, can be best illustrated by a look at what has happened in regard to the development and use of instructional technology.

By the 1970s there was expanding use of technology in administration, in libraries, and in research, and information technology for instruction was being heavily used in the military and in-plant training in industry. But in instruction in higher education, the use of technology lagged far behind.

The Carnegie Commission on Higher Education did a thorough study on instructional technology in higher education in 1972 and produced a report and recommendations in *The Fourth Revolution.*

The publication reported that in 1972 Jarrod Wilcox of MIT did a study among knowledgeable technologists and faculty with the goal of getting predictions about when the then-developed nine technologies would be in routine use. The predictions were that six of the nine would be in routine use before 1980 and that all would be in routine use by 1990. Not even close! The technologies are still not "in routine use," likely because, as the commission stated, faculty tend to be resistant or apathetic toward educational technology. Other contributing factors might be initial high cost, and the lack of training in use of the technologies in doctoral programs.

Some college officials say that a technology-driven restructuring of academe is only five to ten years away. Perhaps, but only as a part of a "public clamor driven" total undergraduate reform movement advocated in this book.

Teaching versus Research

Before the turn of the century, conflict between teaching and research began to appear. The report of the Committee of Fifteen in 1955 stated: "In our national effort of 100 years ago to bring American scholarship up to European standards, it was right . . . to lay special emphasis upon training in research. But by so doing the problems of teaching were neglected."

As was pointed out earlier, in a speech at a national higher education meeting in 1905, Abraham Flexner put it graphically when he said, "the university has sacrificed college teaching at the altar of research."

Also reported earlier, higher education historian W. H. Cowley said that as early as the late 1930s, large numbers of faculty gave their primary allegiance to research and considered teaching a chore to bypass whenever it interfered with their investigations.

So the conflict has raged down through the years. In recent years the research-dominated prestige and reward systems at most institutions have motivated a great many faculty to steal time from teaching and invest it into research.

The justification offered for institutional pressures on every faculty member to be a very active producing researcher is that this is necessary in order for the faculty member to be an effective teacher. This is a myth! A number of research studies have indicated that there is no statistical significant relationship between research productivity and teaching effectiveness. Still, a great many campuses stubbornly maintain research as the dominant and most highly rewarded activity for faculty.

The Academic Program

In the first American colleges every student studied the same series of courses for a degree. By 1886 Harvard introduced the elective system where an undergraduate could earn the A.B. by passing eighteen courses, no two of which needed to be related. This system evolved into a system with a combination of required subjects and electives, which is characteristic of most college and university curriculums as we enter the new millennium.

The Association of American Colleges' report in the mid-1980s said: "As for what passes as a college curriculum, almost anything goes. . . . [W]e are more confident about the length of a college education than its content and purpose."

As a partial explanation for the widespread curricular disarray, the AAC report points out: "Faculty control over the curriculum became lodged in departments that developed into adept protectors and advocates of their own interests at the expense of institutional responsibility and curricular coherence."

A number of thoughtfully prepared plans have been provided to assist institutions to deal with curricular chaos. Three plans of the 1980s—the AAC plan, the Boyer Carnegie plan, and the Cheney *50 Hour* plan—offer somewhat different approaches. The AAC recommendations for types of experiences, Boyer's suggestions of areas of inquiry, and the more prescribed *50 Hour* plan can each be very helpful to faculties and administrators as they seek to provide a framework for a cohesive and meaningful undergraduate curriculum. But the plans have been largely ignored by the academic community.

External Governance

The amount of reassessment and reform of colleges and universities that can take place can depend greatly on external factors. Many institutions of higher education, especially systems of institutions, have protested about external limitations and external intrusion into internal matters.

In the 1977 national meeting of the presidents of the 325 institutions belonging to the Association of State Colleges and Universities, the following resolution was passed:

> . . . the Association believes that excessive state regulation and intrusion into the internal management of colleges and universities are counter-productive and expensive for higher education and the American public as is federal regulation and intrusion.

A number of studies about external governance and relationships were done before and after 1977, including one by Frank Newman in 1987 which found the same concerns as those expressed by the presidents in 1977. Newman concluded that the best institutions developed flexible arrangements with their states or other supervisory bodies that enabled them to develop and operate effectively.

Too many states seem to feel that larger and more powerful external structures will produce more efficient and effective institutions, when just the opposite is more likely true. If colleges and universities are to thoroughly reassess themselves and undergo massive reform, more layers of external management are likely to be a hindrance instead of a help.

However, more lay involvement in reassessment, planning, and implementing reform is important, not to substitute lay judgment for that of academicians, but rather to act as rudders, keeping academicians focused on student and society needs rather than the ambitions of the universities and colleges and the desires of those within the institutions.

Internal Management

Keller's study in the 1980s said the kind of management higher education needs does not yet exist, and a diminished role for faculty in governance and a clearer authority for the executive and more active leadership from management was predicted and recommended.

In *Troubled Times* (1994), Kerr says shared governance between administration and faculty is of declining effectiveness because of increasing faculty default. But, he says, there must be effective governance, and he sees academic administrators—primarily deans and department chairpersons—moving into the void.

So what Keller predicted and recommended more than a decade before was not yet achieved but was being looked to as a likely development in 1994.

Homogenization

In *Reform on Campus* (1972), the Carnegie Commission on Higher Education said that higher education in America had greater diversity than any system in the world, and that the diversity had been one of the greatest strengths and the source of much of the dynamism of the American informal system. The commission report continues: "But recently this trend has been reversed toward homogenization." This means colleges and universities are getting more alike. Reasons for this are discussed in chapter 3 of this book, but as the movement toward homogenization has gained momentum over the years, as recognized by Boyer in *College* in 1987, a predominant reason has been and still is the efforts of a great many nonresearch institutions to emulate the research universities.

One might then deduct that the research university, though unwittingly, is a major factor in the decline of undergraduate education, since the research university emphasizes and exalts research as the 1998 Boyer Commission report points out, and is usually seen as the major culprit in neglecting undergraduate education; and this is the model other institutions are emulating.

Finances

In a 1993 essay in the Wingspread report Gail Promboin warns: "Higher education simply cannot provide what society needs if the average family cannot afford to send its children to college." Promboin explains that between 1975 and 1985, costs to students increased at a rate of 30 percent above inflation.

In the first four years of the 1990s, costs to students rose an average of 50 percent above inflation, and the College Board's annual survey found that in 1995 college tuition rose 6 percent, more than double the rate of inflation. Tuition at public four-year colleges and universities rose 234 percent between 1980–81 and 1994–95, according to a report released in August of 1996 by Congress General Accounting Office. This is unconscionable!

AN OMINOUS UPDATE

Throughout this book there have been discussions of how a great many state universities and colleges have been ripping off their undergraduates in a number of ways. In 2003, runaway state budget deficites across the country are responsible for acceleration of the severity of some of the rip-offs many universities are imposing on their students and prospective students. Several respected news sources recently illustrated the point.

On the July 22 *Lew Dobbs Tonight* CNN TV program, Dobbs and several other contributors bemoaned the severity of the 2003 financial crises in state universities and their failure to seek responsible internal action to alleviate the crises.

CNN correspondent Peter Viles tells Dobbs that this fall, from Albany to Sacramento, legislatures are cutting aid to higher education, and that means tuition hikes. Tuition was raised 39 percent at the University of Arizona, 25 percent at the University of California, 23 percent at Indiana University, 28 percent at the State University of New York, and 30 percent at the University of Virginia.

Colette Sheehy of the University of Virginia points out that higher education is a discretionary part of the state budget, and that there are no mandates about funding higher education as there are for funding Medicaid, K–12 education, or other kinds of state programs.

While tuition increases are considerable this year, Viles reminds us that from 1970 to 2000, the cumulative effect of inflation was that prices rose 353 percent, while tuition, room, and board at state universities rose 531 percent.

Viles explains that higher education has not benefited from increased productivity and has been relatively immune to downsizing; it has not retooled, has not reexamined the way it spends money and the way it provides a service in the way American industry has constantly for three decades.

On the front page of the August 27, 2003, *USA Today*, the following headline blared out over three columns: "Colleges brace for bigger classes and less bang for more bucks." A subhead read, "Though tuition is up, schools cut services." The story by Mary Beth Marklein begins: "It's an axiom among state policymakers: in tough economic times, colleges and universities take the cuts first and hardest. After all, there's always a backup money source: students."

Marklein says further that while double-digit tuition increases have been imposed on the University of Wisconsin twenty-six-campus system (16 percent on the Madison campus), the increases won't make up for an unprecedented $250-million cut in state funding in the state system. At least $100 million will need to be pared from the system's budget. Similar scenarios are unfolding at public universities nationwide.

Public university officials had warned students that they would face larger classes, longer lines, and fewer course options, but only as students returned for the fall term did they begin to grasp the full impact of the financial crises this year. But it is the long-term impact that has some educators on Wisconsin campuses really alarmed.

When adjusted for inflation, the state of Wisconsin is investing less in the system now than it did when the system was created more than thirty years ago. The state portion of the university budget has been cut nearly in half, dropping to 27.3 percent this fiscal year from 49.9 percent in 1973–74, emphasizes Marklein.

On his newscast of September 4, 2003, Tom Brokaw played the same theme: beleagured states are severely cutting funding to higher education, eliminating courses and entire programs, overloading individual classes, and initiating a sharp jump in student costs. One administrator admitted that the education being offered to students at many universities is of declining quality.

In a CNN newscast on September 6, 2003, Aaron Brown said more of the same about what higher education is doing to students, and he quoted a prominent university administrator as predicting even more of the same for students next year.

THE IMPORTANCE OF REFORM

The American public can no longer continue to permit higher education to "fiddle while Rome burns"! The consequences are too frightening.

Consider this: Only about 50 percent of those who begin as freshmen graduate in five years, and an alarming number of those who do graduate are unprepared for the requirements of daily life, especially in the Age of the Learner in the twenty-first century, according to the Wingspread report.

The 1993 National Adult Literacy Survey indicated that surprisingly large numbers of college graduates are unable, in everyday situations, to use basic skills involving reading, writing, computation, and elementary problem-solving, and these findings reflect a significant decline from the 1985 NALS survey. The consequences of more of the same are described thus in the 1994 Wingspread report (see chapter 5):

> A disturbing and dangerous mismatch exists between what American society needs of higher education and what it is receiving. Nowhere is the mismatch more dangerous than in the quality of undergraduate preparation provided on many campuses. The American imperative for the 21st Century is that society must hold higher education to much higher expectations or risk national decline.
>
> Education is in trouble, and with it our nation's hopes for the future. America's ability to compete in a global economy is threatened. The American people's hopes for a civil, humane society ride on the outcome. The capacity of the United States to shoulder its responsibilities on the world stage is at risk.

To prevent further catastrophic decline and deterioration in American society, Americans are going to have to look to education to provide:

- Knowledge and understanding in a mosaic of interconnected major disciplines;
- Basic skills in reading, writing, speaking, listening, computation, technology, problem solving, and lifelong learning;
- One closely knit system from K–12 through higher education, all units working together to meet the needs of students and society;
- A strong emphasis on values throughout the system; and
- Inspired leadership and outstanding performance from higher education—especially undergraduate education—since it has the responsibility of preparing virtually all of the professional personnel for K–12, most of the top leaders in the country, and the core of an informed electorate necessary for the effective functioning of a democracy in a complex society.

BREAKING THE LOGJAM

Undergraduate education in America is suffering from internal debilitating neglect and disrespect, creating the intolerable conditions described in this book. Society desperately needs higher education, with lay input, to do a total and thorough reexamination of undergraduate education's goals, structure, assumptions, procedures, and performance, with the intent of developing and implementing a plan for whatever changes, no matter how massive, are deemed necessary to help undergraduate education achieve maximum efficiency, effectiveness, and affordability.

However, in the last several decades, higher education has shown a virtual indifference to the studies identifying its major problems and the recommendations for solving the problems, showing disdain for, and even resistance to change.

What, then, will it take to break the logjam of higher education's recalcitrance?

The addition of the 1998 Boyer Commission's study further validates many of the criticisms of and recommendations for undergraduate education presented by expert groups and individuals over more than the last two decades. But one more study, even though an excellent one, is not likely to get the job done.

If the badly needed, widespread reform is to be brought about, those in leadership positions—the president, the secretary of education, congressmen, governors, legislators, and others such as Ralph Nader—must lead. They must do two things:

First, fully inform themselves about the essence of the Boyer Commission report and some of the other significant reports mentioned in this book.

Second, forcefully and often describe the woeful condition of much of undergraduate education to the public, and solicit their help in bringing about real reform.

In chapter 5 it was suggested that "the old story about how you get action out of a cantankerous mule seems appropriate here. You whack him over the head with a two-by-four first to get his attention. Hopefully, the surge of outraged protest from all corners of society stimulated by the higher education studies, this book, and courageous exhortations by the aforementioned leaders will be the two-by-four which will get the attention of the academic community so that it can be nudged into a spirited national dialog that will result in a full-scale regeneration of undergraduate education.

"The potential is certainly there. U.S. colleges and universities are collectively a tremendous reservoir of superior intellect and expertise, which has been responsible for establishing world leadership in research, the best graduate schools in the world, and the best professional schools—medicine, engineering, law, etc.

"If that superior intellect and expertise were directed in a totally committed effort toward 'fixing' undergraduate education, it seems a foregone conclusion that U.S. undergraduate education would, in the not too distant future, also be the best in the world, and more than adequately meet the critical needs of students and society."

Let the dialogue begin!

INDEX

229